The
Ten Commandments
of Character

ALSO BY JOSEPH TELUSHKIN

NONFICTION

The Nine Questions People Ask About Judaism
(with Dennis Prager)

Why the Jews?: The Reason for Antisemitism
(with Dennis Prager)

*Jewish Literacy: The Most Important Things to Know
About the Jewish Religion, Its People, and Its History*

*Jewish Humor: What the Best Jewish Jokes Say
About the Jews*

*Jewish Wisdom: Ethical, Spiritual, and Historical Lessons
from the Great Works and Thinkers*

*Words That Hurt, Words That Heal:
How to Use Words Wisely and Well*

*Biblical Literacy: The Most Important People,
Events, and Ideas of the Hebrew Bible*

*The Book of Jewish Values:
A Day-by-Day Guide to Ethical Living*

*The Golden Land: The Story of Jewish Immigration
to America*

FICTION

The Unorthodox Murder of Rabbi Wahl

The Final Analysis of Dr. Stark

An Eye for an Eye

The
Ten Commandments
of Character

ESSENTIAL ADVICE FOR LIVING

AN HONORABLE, ETHICAL,

HONEST LIFE

Joseph Telushkin

BELL TOWER   NEW YORK

Published by Bell Tower, New York, New York.
Member of the Crown Publishing Group,
a division of Random House, Inc.
www.randomhouse.com

Bell Tower and colophon are registered trademarks
of Random House, Inc.

Printed in the United States of America

Design by Meryl Sussman Levavi/Digitext

Library of Congress Cataloging-in-Publication Data
Telushkin, Joseph
    The ten commandments of character / essential advice for living
an honorable, ethical, honest life / Joseph Telushkin.
    1. Ethics, Jewish.   2. Conduct of life.   3. Jewish way of life.
I. Title.
BJ1285 .T44   2003
296.3'6 — dc21   2002154324

ISBN 1-4000-4509-6

10 9 8 7 6 5 4 3 2 1

First Edition

To our beloved friend Annie Fox,
who is a perpetual source of heavenly advice

Acknowledgments

I am pleased to have the opportunity to publicly thank Steve Waldman, the creator of Beliefnet.com, who first developed with me the idea for an ethics advice column. Steve's passion for Beliefnet, and for making available to Americans of all and no religious denominations the insights of dozens of different traditions, has served as an inspiration to me as well. I am also happy to have this chance to thank Paul O'Donnell, my editor at Beliefnet, for his probing, his pushing, and his consistently insightful comments.

David Szonyi, my friend and freelance editor, has worked with me on my last eight books and, as I have often commented, is a blessing to any writer lucky enough to work with him.

There are two other people whom I would like to thank together: Richard Pine, agent extraordinaire, and Toinette Lippe, editor extraordinaire. I have been working with Richard for more than twenty years, and with Toinette for just a few, but they are models of friendship, inspiration, and talent, and both are people of utter integrity. I thank God that they are in my life.

Contents

Preface

As a rabbi, I am heir to a long-standing tradition of advice-giving. Perhaps the Torah's most famous piece of advice was offered in God's name by Moses, near the end of his life: "I have put before you life and death, blessing and curse. Choose life" (Deuteronomy 30:19). As we witness case after case of "suicide bombing" by Palestinian terrorists, or as we remember the nineteen hijackers who struck America on September 11, 2001, we see how difficult it still is for many people to follow the Bible's life-affirming advice.

Several centuries after Moses, when the prophet Samuel was asked by the Israelites to appoint a king, he used all his powers of persuasion to try to dissuade them from instituting a monarchy. He warned them that a king would draft their sons for his own glory or profit (such as fighting his battles or plowing his fields), while their daughters would be put to work as his cooks and bakers. A king would confiscate land and give it to his confederates, and his subjects eventually would "become his slaves" (1 Samuel 8:17). The Israelites ignored Samuel's advice—perhaps the earliest, most penetrating critique in any literature of the injustices perpetrated by kings—and thus suffered the fate that Samuel had predicted.

The biblical book of Proverbs (attributed by tradition to King Solomon) is a compendium of advice, which details, among other things, the importance of avoiding bad company (1:10–19; 4:14–19), being honest in business (3:28), and not being lazy (6:6–11), and even the character traits to look for in a spouse (31:10 ff.).

A thousand years later, the most widely studied book of the Talmud, the Ethics of the Fathers, was compiled. Like Proverbs, this is a compilation of advice, but it is worded in a more practical format. Known in Hebrew as *Pirkei Avot,* the book contains the favorite aphorisms and life lessons of leading rabbis over a period of about four centuries. There you will find many gems that I have passed on to people in this book. They include Hillel's admonition against being too selfless—"If I am not for myself, who will be for me?"—balanced by his warning against becoming egocentric—"And if I am only for myself, what am I?" For an example of how these words should influence our charitable giving and the causes that we should support, see pages 198–199.

There are two more traditions of advice-giving in Jewish religious writings. The first comes from what is known as the Mussar literature, a body of writings and religious counsel that offers insights on how to deal with ethical problems and improve one's character. For example, Rabbi

Yosef Horowitz, founder of the Navorodock school of Mussar, wryly warned his followers not to be impatient, because the process of growth is a slow one: "A person wants to become a scholar and a leader overnight, and to sleep that night as well."

On one occasion, some Jews from Kovno, Lithuania, approached Rabbi Israel Salanter, the Mussar movement's nineteenth-century founder, to seek his counsel. A wealthy Kovno Jew had lost all his money and eventually died of starvation. Although the men who came to Rabbi Salanter had been unaware of the man's desperate financial situation, they felt responsible for his death: How could a man they knew be in such dire circumstances and they remain oblivious to it? What should they do now? Rabbi Salanter advised them that they were not at fault: "That man did not die of hunger. He died of pride. He should have taken charity and not allowed himself to die of hunger."

Yet another source of ethical advice in religious writings is found in what is known as the responsa literature (in Hebrew, she 'elot ve-teshuvot, "questions and answers"). Sometimes, when an ethical or ritual problem arose in someone's life, that person would see no reference to the issue in the Bible or the codes of Jewish law. He or she would seek clarification from a rabbi, who would search out parallels or analogous cases in Jewish law.

While many responsa questions deal with issues of ritual, others confront ethical dilemmas, as in a classic eighteenth-century query directed to Rabbi Ezekiel Landau of Prague. A newly wealthy Jew had acquired an estate with forests and wanted to know whether it was permissible for him to hunt wild animals for sport, provided that he did not eat of the forbidden meat (which was not kosher). The rich man received an answer, along with a reproof: "How can a Jew kill a living thing without any benefit to anyone and engage in hunting merely to satisfy 'the enjoyable use of his time?'" Rabbi Landau went on to note that while the Talmud permits slaying wild animals when they invade human settlements, it is immoral to pursue animals in their own dwelling places in the woods; such activity is "sheer cruelty."

Perhaps the most famous Jewish advice column in modern times was created about a century ago in America's largest-circulation Yiddish newspaper, the *Forward* (there is now an English-language *Forward* as well). Known as the "Bintel Brief," the column originated in January 1906, and readers were invited to submit questions about ethical and personal dilemmas to the paper's editors.

One early question: "I am a socialist, and my boss is a fine man. I know he's a capitalist, but I like him. Am I doing something wrong?" Another interesting question came from a Jew who had been in the United States only five weeks. The man had left behind in Russia a blind father, to whom he had promised to send the first money he earned in America. But he had found it more difficult than he had expected to make money: "Now I want you to advise me what to do. Shall I send my father a few dollars for Passover, or should I keep the little money for myself? In this place, the work will end soon, and I may be left without a job. The question is how to deal with the situation. I will do as you tell me." The editors advised the young man to send the few dollars to his father, because, since he was so young, he would find it easier to earn a living than would his blind father in Russia.

In this book, I have not always followed the traditional norms of Jewish law. For example, the Torah favors sons over daughters in its laws of inheritance, while I'm a firm believer in parents bequeathing to all their offspring equally (see pages 186–195; there are ways in Jewish law to arrange for equal disbursements to all one's children). I also have a more tolerant attitude toward people living together without being married than does Judaism, though I strongly believe in marriage (see pages 253–254), and I believe that people such as Charles Manson, who ordered, but did not personally carry out, the murder of innocent people should be executed (see page 280), though Jewish teachings hold that only those who commit the evil act, and not the person who sent them, should be regarded as fully responsible. Nonetheless, Jewish teachings, more than anything else, have influenced my understanding of human nature, of right and wrong, and of how a decent person should act. Thus, it is Jewish law's understanding of fiscal responsibility that has shaped my conviction that many, though certainly not all, bankruptcies are immoral (see pages 181–182). Likewise, it was a ruling of the twelfth-century philosopher Moses Maimonides that informed my response to a doctor doing a residency, who wanted to know whether it was right for him to apply for food stamps. I explained why I thought it was (based on a text in Maimonides), then offered him a suggestion as to how he could assuage his feelings of guilt (see pages 171–174).

I had long sought a forum in which to apply Judaism's and my understanding of ethics to real-life dilemmas, when I was approached by Steve Waldman, a former editor at *U.S. News & World Report.* Convinced that Americans were ready for a venue where they could learn not only about their own faith, but also about others, he created the website Beliefnet.com, to which dozens of religious scholars and writers contribute columns. I discovered that Steve had been impressed with an earlier book of mine, *Words That Hurt, Words That Heal,* and that it had influenced how he, as a journalist, chose to write about people. From our discussion came the idea for an ethics advice column, and many of the questions and answers found in this book first appeared there.

Letters came in to my column slowly at first, but then in increasing volume. Some months after Beliefnet's launch, a chat room formed around the column, and I had the pleasure of seeing a dozen or more readers arguing with me and one another about the advice I had offered. I learned to get used to some pretty harsh attacks; more gratifying, of course, were letters that indicated that my advice had helped people deal with some serious problems.

So what have I learned in the first two years of trying to present myself as a modern-day Solomon?

1. The Golden Rule, "Do unto others as you will have others do unto you," is still the most helpful guide for figuring out the morally correct solution. It influenced my answers to issues as diverse as whether we have an obligation to correct a bank error (see pages 183–186), to be cautious before passing on a negative rumor (see pages 307–310), and to pay back, if possible, even those personal debts that have been legally forgiven (see page 182).

2. Many people have taught me a lot about ethics. Just before I submitted one column, my friend Charles Mizrahi told me of a new and very different approach to dealing with annoying calls by telemarketers (see pages 231–233). The views of four couples with whom I had dinner in Miami convinced me that my response to one question should be changed (see pages 131–132). And from Beliefnet's chat room, I realized that while it's true that we learn from those with whom we disagree, we can learn as much, if not more, from those with whom we agree. I had counseled a woman who had a male friend whose wife was dying and was increasingly unaware of her surroundings, explaining why it would it would be wrong for her to enter into a sexual relationship with the husband. But readers who agreed with me sent in reasons that had not occurred to me, as to why such behavior would be wrong. Their arguments were powerful, and I was happy to have them in my arsenal (see pages 52–56).

3. A less happy lesson I learned from writing this column is that no matter how clear and fair you think you are being, some people will misunderstand you, and become quite nasty (see pages 239–241 for an example). Such responses taught me that it is best not to be too thin-skinned.

4. The issue most frequently raised is honesty: When is it a virtue? When a vice? I'm referring, of course, not just to financial honesty, although numerous letters came in on that subject (see chapter 5), but also to honesty in relationships. Should one end a relationship with a friend who exaggerates and lies? When is one obliged to give a truthful answer? The Bible teaches that there is a time to speak and

a time to be silent, and plenty of people want guidance as to when each of these is appropriate.

Finally, the writing of this column has repeatedly reminded me of an old truth: Often, the hardest thing in life is not doing the right thing, but knowing the right thing to do.

The
Ten Commandments
of Character

The
Ten Commandments
of Character

If you ask people what they most want from others, they will usually answer "good character" (whether they use precisely this expression or not). The knowledge that those with whom we interact are kind and honorable is the surest guarantee that we and our loved ones will be treated well.

But if you ask people what they want most for themselves, they will answer, "To be happy and successful."

In short, the reason we want good character from others, and happiness and success for ourselves, is that in both cases we want what is best for us.

But what people don't generally realize, as Dennis Prager, the noted radio commentator, has pointed out, is that achieving the good things in life, such as happiness, success, and loving relationships, depends on our developing in ourselves what we most want from others—good character.

Take happiness, for example. Being grateful is not only an important aspect of good character (that's why the word *ingrate* has such a negative connotation), but it is also a prerequisite for leading a happy life. Consider the mind-set of a grateful person: "Look at what so-and-so did for me; he must really care about me. Look how so-and-so helped me; she really loves me." At the very moment a grateful person is cultivating gratitude, she also is cultivating a sense of being loved.

Conversely, think of how an ungrateful person thinks: "The only reason he did that for me is that he wants me to do something for him" or "She helped me because she knows that I know so-and-so, and she thinks I'll intervene with that person for her." By harboring these thoughts, an ungrateful person displays not only a stingy disposition, but also shows how unworthy of love she feels. Ungrateful people can't imagine anybody doing something for them merely out of goodwill and kindness.

Thus, ingratitude turns out to be a major reason ungrateful people are unhappy. Can you think of any ungrateful person whom you know who is happy?

Success also depends in part on developing good character traits. Thus, self-control has long been known as a requisite for leading a moral life (e.g., one has to learn to control one's temper, impulses, or bad inclinations), but we now know that it is equally necessary for leading a success-ful one. Daniel Goleman, author of *Working with Emotional Intelligence,* reports on a study of four-year-olds at Stanford University that became known as the "marshmallow test." Children at the university's preschool were brought into a room one at a time; a marshmallow was put on the table in front of them; and they were told, "You can have this

When the story broke of how Ted Kaczynski was caught, many people condemned David for turning in his brother. The *Los Angeles Times*'s lead op-ed piece claimed that "No one will ever be able to fully trust David Kaczynski." In truth, David Kaczynski, as Dennis Prager has argued, is exactly the kind of person one *can* trust, because he regarded ethical behavior (by stopping future victims from being murdered) as a commitment that overrode loyalty to his brother. Ironically, the one person whose trustworthiness is questionable is the author of this op-ed piece. All we know for certain about him is that if his brother intended to murder you, he wouldn't "betray" his brother by warning you.

The unwillingness to make ethical behavior one's supreme value leads many otherwise admirable people to advocate or do despicable things. Martin Luther, the sixteenth-century founder of Protestantism and the most famous religious reformer in history, believed that faith is more important than ethical behavior. Thus, he held that those who have faith in Jesus will be granted eternal salvation, "even if thousands, thousands of times in one day we should fornicate or murder."

When people consider ethical behavior to be less important than other values, they are apt to lose touch with their hearts. When Jews refused to accept the beliefs that Luther deemed so important, he advocated that their synagogues be burned and their houses destroyed. He also advocated that they be expelled or forced to do physical labor. "I would threaten to cut their tongues out from their throats if they refuse to accept the truth that God is a trinity, not a plain unity," he declared on yet another occasion.

This is what can happen when people elevate other values—even values as noble as family loyalty and faith—above ethical behavior.

3. TREAT ALL PEOPLE WITH KINDNESS, AND WITH THE UNDERSTANDING THAT THEY, LIKE YOU, ARE MADE "IN GOD'S IMAGE"

Among the Bible's most important teachings is that each person is created in God's image (Genesis 1:27). Because every human being contains within him- or herself an aspect of God, each is profoundly important, regardless of the person's education or status in life.

The dreadful things that human beings do to one another often have their origins in people's unwillingness to recognize the sanctity of every human being. Would terrorists plant bombs in public places if they had not first blinded themselves to the fact that the people they kill and maim are, like themselves and their families, created in God's image? Would children taunt and humiliate a weaker, less attractive, or less intelligent peer if they knew and appreciated that he or she, too, is holy and precious to God? All instances of evil—from the Holocaust to the humiliation of a single person—have in common the perpetrator's unwillingness to see the image of God in each human being.

Harold Kushner writes of a story he read in high school about the wife of a British colonel in India who was expecting some prominent guests for tea. As she looked out her front window, she was horrified to see that her gardener had not come and that the front walk was still covered with leaves. Throughout the morning, her annoyance grew. When the man finally arrived, she reprimanded him sharply, calling him ungrateful for not appreciating the good position she had given him. She reminded him how easy it would be to replace him with someone more responsible. When she had finished, he said quietly, "I'm sorry. My little girl died last night, and we had to bury her."

Many of us assess others by how useful they are to us, ignoring the fact that they, no less than we, are creatures made in God's image, with families, hurts, and dreams. That is why it is so important, for example, to display genuine courtesy and gratitude, to see the image of God in waiters, cleaning people, elevator operators, and others who serve us.

Unfortunately, in some professions today, denigrating one's adversaries seems to be encouraged. Defense lawyers commonly regard belittling a prosecution witness as a very effective way to discredit his or her testimony, even when they have reason to believe that the testimony is true. The same applies to political life, in which candidates and campaign managers routinely release embarrassing, but otherwise irrelevant, information about their opponents.

Perhaps most destructive of all, many parents ignore the image of God in their children and use humiliation to try to shock a child into behaving better. Psychiatrist Abraham Twerski describes the excruciatingly painful recollection of a man in his mid-fifties who, during childhood, was a bed wetter. One day, his father announced in the presence of the entire family, "We can't go on vacation and stay in a motel or at friends' homes because you still wet the bed. You are ruining the summer for all of us."

Given that the boy's behavior wasn't willful, it is clear from his father's words (which, fifty years later, still "drove a stake" through the son's heart) that he failed to see his son as a full human being, let alone one created in God's image.

Also, the recognition of the divine image in others guards us against becoming arrogant and believing that we are more worthwhile than others. Because we are all in God's image, it behooves all of us to be humble.

4. BE FAIR

I often ask audiences, "How many of you can think of at least one incident in your life that would be extremely embarrassing to you if it became known to everyone else here?" Almost everyone raises a hand with the exception, I assume, of liars, people with poor memories, and those who have led very boring lives. All of us have done things that we wish to keep hidden, and we would regard anyone who spread such information to others as cruel. Yet when we learn of an embarrassing incident in someone's life, it doesn't usually occur to us how much that person wants the information kept secret; instead, we often share the details with others, perhaps many people. When we do this, do we regard ourselves as mean?

If people were speaking about you as you entered a room, what would you least like to hear them talking about? Most likely, your character flaws and the intimate details of your personal life. Yet, when we speak about other people, isn't that what we often dwell on? Although most of us would claim that the Golden Rule, the most famous rule ever formulated about fairness, is the right way to live one's life, when it comes to speaking about others, most of us violate it almost every day.

Being fair also means not being petty, not judging and dismissing people on the basis of one or two, perhaps uncharacteristic, incidents. Take a story told by William Graf, who served for many years as an assistant to one of the great Hollywood moguls of the 1930s, the man who established Columbia Pictures. The mogul (whose name I am omitting out of a sense of fairness) once fired a carpenter who had worked at the studio for more than twenty-five years because the man had been caught taking home a hammer belonging to the company. Graf argued on the carpenter's behalf, but the mogul was adamant: "Fire him! He's a crook. He's a thief."

Sometime later, the two men passed the carpenter on a street corner where he was selling papers. After they walked by, the mogul said to Graf, "Did you see the crook there?" When Graf answered, "The man is not a crook for a dollar-eighty [the value of the hammer]," the mogul snapped, "I told you never to mention that again."

Was the carpenter wrong for taking the hammer? Of course. But did his employer treat this twenty-five-year employee fairly? Certainly not—I doubt if the mogul would have wanted to have all his achievements ignored and be condemned as a thief had he once cheated someone out of $1.80.

The essence of being a fair person is not to be petty, but to judge people by all they've done, and not seek to diminish their status by one or two bad things you know about them. For example, in a feminist journal, I once saw a critique of Oskar Schindler, focusing on his reputation as a womanizer. Schindler was, in fact, a womanizer. But the far larger, and more relevant, truth about Schindler is that he repeatedly risked his life during World War II to save more than 1,100 Jews from certain death.

In truth, I wonder if the writer would have displayed Schindler's courage and ingenuity in saving lives. And if she wouldn't have—and few of us would have—would it not have behooved her to write in a fairer manner about a person who was her—and my—ethical superior?

5. BE COURAGEOUS

We generally think of physical bravery when the word *courage* is mentioned. We picture a soldier in battle, a fire-fighter walking into a burning building, or someone in a totalitarian society hiding an innocent dissident, knowing that the punishment for such an act might well be death. Fortunately, such courage and heroism is rarely required of most of us.

A second, more common, type of courage is moral courage, the willingness to face social disapproval in order to do what is morally right. While it would seem self-evident that moral courage should be easier to carry out than physical, the opposite is the case. A character in Vietnam veteran Tim O'Brien's book *The Things They Carried* recalls an incident that happened when he was ten. A girl in his class, whom he "adored," was dying of a brain tumor. Her head had been shaved, and she wore a scarf to school to cover it. A class bully started tugging at the scarf, and eventually succeeded in pulling it off. Confused and ashamed, the other boy stood by silently, watching the girl's misery but doing nothing: "I should've stepped in; fourth grade is no excuse. Besides, it doesn't get easier with time, and twelve years later, when Vietnam presented much harder choices, some practice at being brave might've helped a little."

In O'Brien's account of his Vietnam experiences, *If I Die in a Combat Zone,* he relates how the lack of moral courage allowed a group of American soldiers to acquiesce in an act of sadism. On a hot day, an American company had stopped in a village, where an old, blind farmer helped them to shower. He drew up water from a well and poured it over the soldiers. His manner was pleasant, and he smiled and laughed with the troops. Then, one of the men, for no reason, threw a carton of milk at the old man and hit him in the head, hurting him. The other soldiers lacked the moral courage to do anything, or even to say words of reproof, to the man who had behaved so badly.

6. BE HONEST

A two-thousand-year-old talmudic text *(Shabbat* 31a) teaches that the first question people are asked after they die is not "Did you believe in God?" or "Did you observe Judaism's rituals?" but "Were you honest in your business dealings?" What matters most to God, and therefore what should matter most to us, is not issues of faith or ritual observance, but honesty in our dealings with others.

In the letters that come to my column, I receive more questions about honesty than any other subject. These questions include several that are discussed in this book (see, for example, chapter 5).

People must be able to rely on your honesty in many different areas: Can they trust you in money matters? Can they trust you to be truthful? And when, if ever, is it moral to be untruthful?

7. BE GRATEFUL

The character trait that offers the most immediate reward to its practitioner is gratitude. As noted earlier, being grateful is a prerequisite for happiness (see pages 23–24).

Are those who are willing to acknowledge all the good done for them Pollyannaish and naive? No. Although ungrateful people may refuse to acknowledge this fact, there are many good people in the world. My wife and I were visiting a man who had been diagnosed with Lou Gehrig's disease. Although confined to a wheelchair, he still had some physical strength and managed to visit Israel. While describing his trip, he teared up when he told us of how each time he had needed to go down steps to get to a restaurant or a tourist site, people had volunteered to carry him in his wheelchair.

In addition to revealing meanness, ingratitude often indicates that a person is capable of great evil (i.e., if somebody is not nice to people who have been good to him, one can imagine how unnice he will be to everyone else). Consider the case of Martin Heidegger, who is widely regarded as a great philosopher—perhaps the twentieth century's greatest. In 1928, early in Heidegger's career, his mentor, Edmund Husserl, pushed through Heidegger's appointment to a chair in philosophy at the University of Freiburg. Five years later, when the Nazis came to power, Husserl was forced out of the university because he was a Jew. The university's rector resigned, in part to protest Husserl's dismissal. But Heidegger donned a swastika and took over the rector's post. Several years later, when Heidegger republished his classic work, *Being and Time,* he removed his earlier dedication of the book to Husserl. When Husserl died, Heidegger neither attended the funeral nor sent a note to Husserl's widow. A great philosopher, but an ingrate, Heidegger became the most prominent intellectual to become a Nazi, an act for which, not surprisingly, he never apologized.

8. PRACTICE SELF-CONTROL

The wrongs committed by truly evil people—the Hitlers, Stalins, and Pol Pots of the world—emanate, in large measure, from their lack of conscience. The wrongful acts committed by the rest of us generally emanate from a lack of self-control. Once someone chooses not to exercise control, he may well end up justifying whatever he wants to do. In his novel *The Fall,* Albert Camus describes the mind-set of such a person: "My sensuality . . . was so real that even for a ten minute adventure, I'd have disowned my mother and father. . . . I had principles, to be sure, such as that the wife of a friend is sacred. But I simply ceased quite sincerely, a few days before, to feel any friendship for the husband."

Many people rationalize that they can't control their

temper or how they act when enraged. This is precisely the excuse offered by defenders of the great World War II military hero George Patton. Patton ordered a mule that had gotten in the way of his jeep to be shot, and forced members of an antiaircraft unit to stand at attention for being sloppily dressed, despite the fact that they had just beaten off an attack and some of the men were wounded. In one notorious incident, he slapped a hospitalized, shell-shocked soldier, and denounced the man for being a coward. Patton's commander, General Dwight D. Eisenhower, did not believe that Patton lacked self-control, only that he was refusing to practice it. He ordered Patton to publicly apologize for slapping the soldier, put Patton on probation, and postponed his promotion to general. After this, there were no reports that Patton committed more acts of emotional or physical abuse during the two remaining years of World War II. In other words, Patton—and just about every other person with a bad temper—could control himself when motivated to do so.

9. EXERCISE COMMON SENSE

People generally regard common sense as a pragmatic, not a moral, trait. Thus, we assume that a person with common sense will know the right way to conduct herself in a social setting and will have an intuitive sense of whether another person is trustworthy.

In truth, a lack of common sense frequently results in immoral or hurtful behavior, both on the individual and the national level. For example, in one of the first letters sent to my column (see page 234), a woman wrote to tell me this: "At a party a few months ago, when I was barely beginning to come to terms with the reality that my two-month-old baby was born with a severe disability, I mentioned my situation to another guest at the party. She replied, 'You must be a very nice person—I don't believe that God would give such a baby to someone who wasn't good enough to take care of him.' I was stunned, hurt, appalled, and angry."

Was the woman who offered this comment a malicious, cruel person? Absolutely not. Her intentions were good, and her desire was to be kind. Unfortunately, she lacked common sense, and this resulted in a kindly intention becoming a thoughtless and hurtful act. The implication of her words was that the better a person you are, the more likely it is that God will reward you by sending you a baby with disabilities. Such a viewpoint might actually make good people regret their goodness, while discouraging others from wanting to do good. For that matter, how would the woman who offered this comment feel if someone said to her, "You seem like such a nice person that I am sure God will reward you by causing you to have many babies with special needs"?

Similarly, someone with a lack of common sense has the capacity to inflict terrible things on large numbers of people, not just individuals. To provide one illustration: England was led during World War II by Prime Minister Winston Churchill, who galvanized and inspired the British in their war against the Nazis. At the same time, perhaps the second-most-famous man in the British Empire was Mahatma Gandhi, a man regarded by many as the pre-eminent moral leader of the twentieth century.

Gandhi possessed in abundance many of the traits that comprise the Ten Commandments of character. He was a man of great courage—indeed, he was fearless; he also exercised extraordinary self-control and was punctiliously honest. However, what Gandhi, a believer in absolute pacifism, lacked was common sense. How else can one explain his widely publicized advice to the soldiers of England in the spring of 1940—at a time when Hitler's troops were conquering country after country in Europe—to lay down their weapons and let Hitler occupy England and all the countries Germany had invaded? Had Gandhi, and not Churchill, led England, the result would have been that almost every Jew in the world would have been murdered by the Nazis, and hundreds of millions of other people would have been forced to live under the most totalitarian and brutal regime in history.

It has been wisely said that "common sense is not common." How unfortunate!

10. ADMIT WHEN YOU HAVE DONE WRONG, SEEK FORGIVENESS, AND DON'T RATIONALIZE BAD BEHAVIOR

When I first drafted this list of commandments, I wrote this last commandment as "Don't rationalize, but admit when you have made a mistake." I soon realized that formulating it that way would itself be a mistake.

It has become all too fashionable for people to do things that are wrong and, when caught, to apologize for having made a mistake. Several years ago, in a case that received national publicity, two high-school students murdered their newborn baby. When caught, the couple apologized for their "mistake."

Of course, as Dennis Prager has pointed out, their statement was self-serving and nonsensical. You make a mistake when you intend to do something that is right, and then, because of an accident, something else, perhaps something terrible, happens. But this couple didn't kill their baby by accident. What they did wasn't a mistake, it was a great wrong.

Blaming what you have done on a mistake, your poor upbringing, or the bad influence of others is the most common way of not accepting responsibility for your actions. Psychologist Bruno Bettelheim, summarizing an important insight he gained about human behavior during the year he spent as a prisoner in the Buchenwald and Dachau concentration camps, concluded, "Blaming others, or outside conditions, for one's own misbehavior may be the child's privilege; if an adult denies responsibility for his own actions, it is another step towards personality disintegration."

People of character, knowing that they possess free will, acknowledge when they have done something wrong. It is this acknowledgment that motivates them to seek out those whom they have hurt, ask forgiveness, and devote themselves to doing better in the future.

When one who has done wrong admits to making a mistake, and nothing more, he is committing a second serious mistake, one that will prevent him from developing a deep and worthwhile character.

ONE

Family

Dear Joseph,

My boyfriend is a Catholic, and I am a Buddhist. To me, this is absolutely no problem. Recently, however, he told me that we cannot get married unless I get baptized. I am more than willing to do so, but isn't that hypocritical? The more I think about this, the more I wonder: What sort of religion is it that decrees that two people who love each other so much should not be allowed to marry based on their feelings? I could really use some guidance.

Annoyed

Dear Annoyed,

There are many considerations that people make in deciding whether they want to marry someone. For example, a man might think that a woman is the best friend he's ever had, a wonderful person, and potentially a great mother, but conclude that he's not sufficiently attracted to her to marry her. Is such a decision immoral or hypocritical? I don't think so, even thought the woman might be a lovely person.

For your boyfriend, to share a religious faith with his wife seems to be as critical as being sexually attracted to her, and I therefore don't see his demand as necessarily hypocritical. But I find it disturbing that he focuses purely on the act of baptism, the implication being that you should go through a mechanical act in which you don't believe. It would make more sense if he asked you to study Catholicism, then decide whether or not you want to convert.

If you choose not to, then it's a good thing he made you aware now of how much this issue matters to him. And if you choose to end the relationship, it probably would be wise for your boyfriend to date only Catholic women in the future rather than to go out with women to whom he is attracted and then spring this demand on them. (To be fair to him, it is possible that he might not have realized, until your relationship had progressed this far, how important his Catholic faith was to him.)

Dear Joseph,

I'm a Jewish woman married to a Christian man. When we met eight years ago, it became clear that I was not going to convert to Christianity, and he had no intention of becoming a Jew. His religion matters to him a great deal, as mine does to me. He did agree, however, that our children would be raised as Jews. With that understanding in mind, I happily agreed to marry him. Now, we have three children. The oldest, a girl, turned six, and I brought her to register at the Hebrew school of a local synagogue. My husband became very upset and told me that what I was doing was destroying him; he feels, he said, like an outsider in his own home. In other words, he wants to go back on our agreement and not have us favor either religion. "When they grow up, they'll choose" is his new attitude. Now I'm the one who's very upset. Shouldn't he be bound by what he told me before we married? I feel cheated and . . .

Betrayed

Dear Betrayed,

I suspect that intermarriages are most apt to succeed when a noncommitted Christian marries a noncommitted Jew. In such a case, because religion is not particularly important to either parent, it is unlikely to become a source of conflict and distress; whatever religion or nonreligion their children choose won't usually be emotionally disturbing to the couple.

A second type of intermarriage that has a better-than-average chance of succeeding is when one of the partners is committed to his/her religion, and the other is not religious. Thus, a noncommitted Jew or

Christian might not be upset to see his or her child raised in another religion, since that person has little, if any, connection to the religion in which he or she was reared.

But your situation presents a built-in difficulty. Each of your religious commitments matter to you, and so you're going to care that your children share in a tradition that you find meaningful. That your husband agreed, prior to your marriage, to raise your children as Jews only suggests to me that he probably didn't think through how important having children would be to him, and how vital it would be for them to share holidays, faith, and church with him. When he made the agreement, he loved you and wanted to satisfy your need. Now, eight years later, he finds that the agreement is too painful, and that it runs the risk of making him feel alienated from his children.

Do you have the right to insist that he abide by what he said? I suppose so, but if you do, your marriage may be fraught with increasing tension. As I'm sure you are aware, your children are Jewish (according to Jewish law) since, in Judaism, the religious identity of the mother determines that of the children. But if having your children strongly identify as Jews is important to you, then following your husband's suggestion will be upsetting for you, since it is likely to lead to your children becoming Christian. It has been repeatedly noted that if there is no preference expressed in the household for one religion, when children mature, they tend to follow the religion more dominant in their society. If you and your children lived in Israel, your children would most probably opt to identify as Jews; in the United States, as Christians. Except, perhaps, if they have a stronger sense of identification with the parent who belongs to the minority religion. But do you really want to try and create a situation where your children love and identify with you more than with your husband, and therefore choose Judaism?

In short, I know of no good solution to your dilemma other than to note that when people with different and strongly held religious commitments marry and have a family, they often add an unresolvable tension to their marriage.

Dear Joseph,

I'm a twenty-two-year-old woman dating a man who is five years older than me. He works in money management and is very successful. He's generous and showers me with gifts. He also listens carefully and seems to take me seriously. But he has one trait that annoys me: He's not nice to service people, such as waiters, taxi drivers, or doormen. For example, when he orders in a restaurant, his tone is very demanding, and he doesn't say "please" or "thank you." I challenged him on it once, and he said that you don't have to say "please" and "thank you" when a person's just doing his job. My mother and a few of my friends think I'm exaggerating the significance of this, but this behavior concerns me.

Worried in Brooklyn

Dear Worried in Brooklyn,

It should concern you. There's a good chance that if you marry this man—three years from now; five, if you're lucky—you'll find out that when you do what he expects his wife to do, like beautifully decorating your home or preparing an excellent dinner, you won't be entitled to a thank-you, either. Years ago, my friend Dennis Prager started advising listeners to his talk show thus: "When you go out on a date, it's more important to see how your date treats the waitress than how he [or she] treats you. Since it's important at a relationship's beginning for your date to make a good impression on you, he will treat you well. But how he treats the waitress will reflect how he's going to treat you once he can take your love for granted."

I believe that the best guideline on what character trait to look for first in a spouse was set down more than three thousand years ago in the Book of Genesis. In chapter 24, Eliezer, Abraham's trusted servant, is dispatched to the town of Nahor to find a wife for Abraham's son, Isaac. When Eliezer arrives, he stops at the town's well just as the local women are coming out to draw water. Eliezer prays for a divine sign by which he can choose the right bride for Isaac: "Let the maiden to whom I say, 'Please, lower your jar that I may drink,' and who replies, 'Drink, and I will also water your camels,' let her be the one whom You have decreed for Your servant Isaac" (Genesis 24:14). Shortly thereafter, Rebecca arrives at the well, and not only offers Eliezer water, but also brings water for the thirsty camels (no small task, given that a camel can drink up to twenty gallons).

The trait that clearly distinguishes Rebecca is kindness. Seeing a thirsty man and thirsty animals, her immediate desire is to relieve their plight. And while our contemporary urban society hardly lends itself to precisely this sort of test, what remains relevant is Eliezer's awareness of kindness as the supreme virtue in a spouse.

If you truly believe that, except for this trait, this relationship has potential, then you must communicate to your boyfriend that kindness to others, including those he regards as his social inferiors, is very important to you; indeed, as far as you're concerned, lack of such kindness will be a deal breaker. Tell him that you don't want to raise children with a man who will teach them, both by word and example, that there are classes of people to whom one does not owe courteous behavior.

If this man's bad manners are deeply embedded in his personality and not susceptible to change, then you will be better off without him. I know you mention that he is very successful. In current American parlance, the word *successful* has but one meaning: "money." For example, if someone makes a lot of money—even if he or she has few friends and a dysfunctional family life—we call that person successful. Conversely, if someone makes little money, but has a beautiful family life, we call that person unsuccessful. What a narrow view of success. If you want to have a truly successful life, by which I mean a life imbued with goodness, love, and respect, marry a person who expresses those feelings toward *all* people.

Postscript: A reader wrote to tell me that the central point I was making to Worried in Brooklyn was set down in a song, "Rule Number One," by singer/songwriter David Wilcox. As Wilcox tells listeners at the song's beginning, "One day, you are the waiter."

Dear Joseph,

I have a moral dilemma. I have been close friends for six years with a married man whose wife was diagnosed one year ago with terminal brain cancer. For the past year she has been aphasic, unable to communicate. She's now deteriorating and doesn't have much time left. In a sense, he lost her a year ago. The man and I have always had a strong mutual attraction as well as a deep, immediate friendship, but we never crossed the line into an affair. In the past few months he has told me he'd like to start a relationship with me, including being physical (I am single). He doesn't see any reason to wait—he is lonely, grieving, and has no close relationship now that his wife is no longer available to him. I have strong feelings for him, and even sense that we may be destined to be together. I am very torn about this because while I care for him deeply, another part of me feels that to act on these feelings now would be somehow morally obscene. I believe that we both genuinely care for one another, and he is in great emotional need while his life is falling apart. They have three fairly young children. I would be grateful for your comments.

In a Dilemma

Dear In a Dilemma,

As they say in Yiddish, "Oy vey." The situation you describe is so sad, and if you decide to allow your relationship with this man to turn at this time into an affair, I would not condemn you as acting in a "morally obscene" manner. But, having said that, I strongly feel that you should wait. You write that the sick woman "does not have much time left." Then why rush matters, and commit what is still an act of adultery? You also note that the couple has three young children. Since it seems distinctly possible that you and this man will eventually wed, I believe you will make possible a far better relationship with your future stepchildren if it's clear that you and their father did not carry on a romantic relationship while their mother was dying. If they come to know that the two of you had done so, I suspect that you will find your relationship with them will be damaged, perhaps permanently.

You write in your letter that "I have strong feelings for him, and even sense that we may be destined to be together." If this is true, then that's all the more reason not to rush matters, since the two of you will probably have many years together.

To start a physical relationship now is wrong for yet another reason. This man is still the one in charge of making medical decisions about his wife. There is something very unseemly, to say the least, about the one making such decisions being already involved in an intimate relationship with another woman.

You write that you have been close friends with this man for six years, during five of which his wife was in good health. From the tone of your letter, it sounds like the strong mutual attraction existed even before the woman became ill. You exercised restraint then, and I believe you should exercise it now. Be there for your friend emotionally, but not physically.

Postscript: My answer to In a Dilemma prompted more responses than anything else I've written. With few exceptions, the many respondents opposed the writer's entering into a sexual relationship with her friend.

One writer's reasoning came in the form of a warning that was as pragmatic as it was ethical: "Ultimately, should you proceed with your intended affair, you may find yourself out in the cold. For you will certainly be a source of guilt for this man sooner or later."

Several writers focused more than I had on the potential hurt to the children: "Of course they will find out or figure it out. If they don't, someone else will, and will eventually tell them. Count on it. If she wants them to love and trust her, she'll hold on a little longer."

One reader shared a painful recollection "from the trenches": "My father cheated on my mother while she was dying of breast cancer. I was in my mid-thirties at the time. My father's relationship with my soon-to-be stepmother (whom he married within a year of my mother's death) completely eliminated his ability to be a comfort to my mother, as well as my sisters and me, not only up to the point where she died, but for a long while afterward. It also affected my mother's will to live. Our family's entire stability and harmony (including my father's) were sacrificed for many years because of this. This was one of the most painful things I have ever experienced, all at the hands of someone who professed to love me, my dad. It has taken me many years to rebuild a relationship with him. I hope this helps guide your decision."

Other writers emphasized that adultery, even when one's spouse is very ill, is still adultery. One correspondent wrote of a similar case she had read about: "The man's friend was telling him he 'should get on' with his life, even while his wife was on her deathbed. The friend said, 'Why shouldn't you start dating again? Your wife doesn't even know who you are!' The husband's response was, 'No, she doesn't know who I am, but I know who she is. She's my wife.'" The writer concluded, "She had been a loving and faithful wife and mother, and he wasn't going to break his covenant to her or to God, just because he was lonely. That is a real man."

There's no principle more basic to me in ethics than

the Golden Rule. I hadn't thought to apply it here, but one of my readers did: "I've always followed the rule that, when in doubt, put yourself in another's shoes. If the woman concerned about the relationship were dying now, how would she feel if she knew her husband was having an affair now and planning a marriage as soon as she kicked the bucket? We're not talking someday after she is dead and gone; we're talking immediately. How would you feel if you were dying and losing your husband to another woman at the same time?"

Dear Joseph,

My husband and I have been married for twenty-four years and have two teenage children. Until recently, we were prominent and respected members of the small Jewish community in our city. However, nearly two years ago, my husband told me he no longer loved me and had found a soul mate— another woman with whom he wished to spend the rest of his life. He'd been having an affair with her for some time and wished to start a new life with her. I was completely shocked, and our family was thrown into turmoil and despair. Unfortunately, the community found out about his "dalliance," and his affair is now the preferred subject of gossip. We have been to marriage counselors, and we've seen therapists separately. So far he hasn't moved out of the house, but only into another bedroom. He says he still intends to move out but the time isn't right. I have been trying to preserve the marriage, but he won't tell me whether he still loves this other woman or even what his relationship with her now is.

The main reason he's still in the house is because our teenage daughter has been terribly affected by this whole event. Until this happened, she worshipped her father. I'm waiting for him to say he's sorry for what has occurred, but all he says is that he's sorry he's hurt me, but not sorry for what he's done. I've worked so hard to create a family, and I don't want to see it destroyed. Some people say I should stay and keep trying. Just tell me: Purely on moral grounds, should I keep working at preserving the family, or should I kick the b—— out?

Confused

Dear Confused,

I truly sympathize with how devastated you must feel. I strongly believe that it is worth trying to save a marriage when there is a marriage left to save. However, in this case, since your husband isn't even willing to express remorse for what he has done, and leaves you no reason to assume he won't act in the same way in the future, he is giving you little to work with.

You say that some of your friends are encouraging you to try to keep your marriage together. Their advice might be more revealing about them than helpful to you. A woman once told me that when she started confiding in friends about her unhappy marriage, she found that those who were happily married advised her to leave her husband (the thought of remaining with someone who mistreated and/or didn't love them seemed too awful to contemplate). Meanwhile, those who themselves had unhappy marriages were threatened by the idea of her divorcing, since such a move would force them to reconsider the decision they had made to try to preserve their problematic marriages.

Finally, you must ask yourself if the current relationship models a healthy marital relationship for your daughter. What is the lesson you wish to convey to her? That she should stay married even if her spouse tells her that he doesn't love her, but loves someone else? I'm sure this is not the future you wish for your daughter, nor is it one you should wish for yourself. You deserve better.

A final thought: Since I have not heard your husband's account of what has transpired, I must emphasize that what I have said is applicable only if the situation as you have described it is fully accurate. If, for example, he is more repentant about what has happened than you have conveyed, and if he wants to work at saving your marriage, then, of course, my answer would be different.

Postscript: Confused's letter provoked an enormous number of responses, and their advice was uniform—get out of the relationship: "You need to worry about yourself, not your family right now," one reader suggested. "Your family will survive, a little bit differently than before, but they will survive. You may not if you do not take the time to be concerned about your own mental well-being. The humiliation of being the object of town gossip when you did nothing wrong is difficult to deal with. Don't continue to fight to save a marriage where the partner simply wants out. . . . Be kind to yourself, you are a child of God."

Yet another reader reminded Confused that "being moral doesn't mean being stuck in a relationship based on deceit."

Dina shared her perspective that "as a daughter of divorce, I must say that the longer a couple stays married for 'the sake of the children' and not for themselves (which seems to be what Confused is doing), the harder it is for the children to (1) deal with the actual divorce when it happens and (2) have normal relationships in life. My own father lived in the house in a different room for a year while my parents were deciding whether or not to divorce. I have more emotional scars from that year than any other. It becomes easier for children when we are not exposed to our parents' mutual lack of respect for each other on a daily basis."

Dear Joseph,

I am a millionaire by gift from my family. When I married, I insisted that my wife, who was poor but hardworking, accept as a gift half of the value of the home that I had purchased for us to live in. She had a difficult time accepting this gift, but I insisted. Over the years she worked hard to transform our home. Now I am divorcing and can legally deny my wife part of the wedding gift. I am angry about giving her money, as I have fed and sheltered her for years and also provided her with spending money. Is it O.K. to take back part of my gift?

Don't Want to Be a Sucker

Dear Don't Want to Be a Sucker,

I suspect you know the right thing to do: Let your soon-to-be-ex-wife keep the value of her half of the house. True, you're angry at your wife now, and perhaps you feel she has taken advantage of you financially, but you also acknowledge that she wasn't greedy. After all, you had to convince her to accept half of the house. You also acknowledge that she worked hard to transform the house, thereby increasing its value.

I once heard the singer Diana Ross say of her divorced spouse, "Anyone I once loved a lot, I still love a little." Perhaps you're not feeling any love now. But for the sake of the love you once felt, act generously. Also, if you try to deny her half of the value of the house, you probably will also have to deny that you once promised her that half as a gift. To do so would involve you in a serious lie, possibly under oath, as well as in an act of extreme mean-spiritedness. You gave this woman your word, and I hope you are the sort of person who takes pride in being "a man of his word." That is a trait worth taking pride in. Don't change the sort of person you are, just because of a desire for money and revenge.

✻

Dear Joseph,

As a gay man who has been in a conventional marriage for twenty years (most of them very happy), I would be grateful for your perspective on a dilemma I have yet to resolve: What are my ethical obligations to my wife in this matter? If honesty is the bedrock of a marriage, how can I not discuss a realization as basic as a profoundly changed awareness of my sexuality? But given the inevitable devastation that will result, is it self-indulgent not to "swallow bitterness" (as the Chinese put it) and just continue with a relationship that is something of a charade? My coming out would be by choice, there is no third party involved, and I have not been involved in any extramarital relationship up to this point.

Uncertain

Dear Uncertain,

If you've been bisexual in orientation until now, and have lived for two decades in a relationship that's been "very happy," your first obligation is to try to see if you can still make this relationship work. Your letter's implication is that your spouse would be shocked and devastated to learn that you were leaving her because you regard yourself as homosexual.

This suggests that until now you have been a sufficiently ardent heterosexual so that she has no clue concerning your other sexual orientation. If that is the case, then perhaps your relationship need not end.

On the other hand, if you intend from now on to choose to follow an exclusively homosexual identification and lifestyle (and I deliberately use the word *choose,* for whereas someone who is solely homosexual doesn't have a choice, your decades of heterosexual activity suggest that you do), then it would seem that you have the obligation to share this information with your spouse. For one thing, adultery means having sex with someone other than one's spouse, so that if you intend to start engaging in sex with men, your spouse needs to know that. Presumably, she won't consent to live in an "open marriage" (there are health risks involved, of course, as well). Therefore, the moment it becomes clear to you that your life as an exclusively heterosexual male is over, you're morally obligated to tell your wife. In any case, if you no longer have heterosexual feelings, your wife will pick up on this, and then you will no longer be the only one "swallowing bitterness."

What makes your letter particularly difficult to answer is the almost casual way you remark on the fact that most of the years of your marriage were very happy. You see, I have long felt that it is very bad for everyone—heterosexuals and homosexuals alike—when society discriminates against gays, because, among other reasons, such discrimination causes many gay people to try to live publicly heterosexual lives (e.g., getting married), and such a falsification of their sexual identity can lead to misery both for themselves and for their heterosexual partners. To put it more bluntly, I would not want one of my daughters to marry a homosexual man who marries either because he is ashamed of his homosexuality or because he fears the social or professional consequences if it becomes public knowledge. Women who have married such men, and I know several, have found the experience very painful, starting with the fact that living with men who regard heterosexual relations as burdensome makes them feel unattractive and unsatisfied. (I also know men whose hearts have been shattered by wives who informed them that they were getting a divorce so that they could live as lesbians.)

But your case is different. You don't explain how it came about that what was acceptable to you for so many years has now become unacceptable. Therefore, before you give up on something that has brought you much happiness to experiment with something that might not prove as fulfilling (you indicate that you're not coming out because of an already-existent partner, so you have no idea how it will work out), you should think this matter through long and hard. Throwing away what has been good because of what might turn out to be a passing phase could be the sort of error that causes great pain and no gain.

Postscript: I received a poignant response from a gay man who had come out, and had encountered the kind of "helpers" whom anyone in need of advice should avoid:

"I know a few men who are gay (as am I) who are married to women and secretly meet other men. Don't go down that road. It's a miserable existence. One lie leads to another and another. Eventually, you'll live in fear that your whole lying house of cards will come crashing down. The closet is a terrible place to be. . . . I think the worst thing is trying to go through something like this alone. Just beware of 'helpers' whose antigay, or pro-gay, agenda is more important to them than your real problems. If you must meet other men, then you have no choice but to be honest with your wife and face the consequences, and you have to ask yourself if it's worth it. For me, coming out and being honest was the most painful, heart-wrenching thing I ever did, and ultimately the most rewarding, because now everyone knows who I am and I no longer live in fear."

Dear Joseph,

I'm in my late sixties now, and I have terminal cancer. I'm also carrying a terrible secret. My husband and I have two children, a girl and a boy, both in their thirties. Our son, though, is not my husband's, though he doesn't know this. It all happened during a brief affair at a time of bad tension in our marriage. The affair turned out to be inconsequential, and the man himself is long dead. I love my husband, and yet the thought that I'm dying with this lie between us gives me no peace. I feel that I should speak to him and tell him, and my son, the truth.

In Deep Pain

Dear In Deep Pain,

My heart goes out to you, both for the pain of knowing that you have terminal cancer and for the secret that you're carrying with you. But I plead with you to say nothing. What is this great truth that you wish to bequeath to your son? That the man he thinks of, and loves, as his father is biologically not so? What good can come from telling *this* truth at *this* time?

Imagine how you'll feel going to your grave knowing the pain you've left behind, and how both your husband and son will live the rest of their lives with this sense of loss and betrayal. In the distant past, you did something wrong, and now you want two innocent victims of your action to be the ones to suffer. You must ask yourself why you didn't tell the truth to your husband many years ago, when he could have chosen to act on this truth (perhaps by divorcing you). To have lived with him all these years and then "unload" this truth on him now would, in my view, be a worse betrayal of him than was your earlier act of adultery.

My thoughts and prayers are with you. And for your husband's sake and your son's sake, please, please say nothing.

✌

Dear Joseph,

My brother and his wife are drawing up their will and have told me that in the event both of them die, they want to appoint my husband and me to be their children's legal guardians, and to raise them. How can I say no to my brother? He and his wife have four children under the age of nine, and I am his only sibling. In addition, his wife's siblings would be inappropriate as parents. My husband, however, is very uncomfortable about assuming such a responsibility. For one thing, he points out, the financial implications are immense. A financial-service institution told me that I could project expenses of about $150,000 per child. My husband regards this figure, which admittedly is a lot of money, as naively low. As he reminds me, if we add on four children to our household, we'll need a considerably larger house, and given that we send our two children to private school (my brother sends his to public), we would feel uncomfortable not sending them to a private school as well. My husband is also far from certain that he wants to raise these children. What should I say to my brother?

Highly Uncomfortable

Dear Highly Uncomfortable,

There are times in life that requests are made of us to which it is pretty much impossible to say no, and yet our yes might not be all that wholehearted. Indeed, I suspect that many people agree to be legal guardians for someone else's children largely because they're certain that the tragic scenario that would require them to do so—both parents' deaths—won't come to pass. On the other hand, if such a horrific event happens, many people might find that they'd be willing to step in and do the right thing, as self-sacrificial as it might be.

I would ask you to pose this question to your husband: "Should I tell my brother that if both he and his wife die, you would rather that they send the children to an orphanage, but that you promised to visit occasionally? Or alternatively, should I tell him that you're willing to assume responsibility for the two children you like best, and that he should try to find different homes for the other two?"

When phrased in such a manner, it obviously becomes difficult to reject your brother's request without causing a significant cooling or rupture in your relationship with him. Of course, you could say no in a less-provocative manner ("We're just uncomfortable assuming such a responsibility"), but the effect would be much the same as if you gave the answer above. Your brother is likely to reason, "So what do they expect to happen to my children if my wife and I die? After all, if my own sister's husband is not willing to let them into their house, who, other than an institution, will be willing?"

Having said this, let me add that I believe that your husband's financial concerns are reasonable. You would need a new, much larger house, and there is the issue of private-school tuition while the children are young. Later, if the children go to private colleges, tuition could amount to well over a hundred thousand dollars for each child. Given this, and assuming that your brother and wife are in good health and can obtain term insurance at reasonable rates, I don't think it unfair of you to ask that they take out $1.5 million to $2 million in life insurance. From what I understand, because the deaths of both parents at this stage in their lives is so unlikely, such insurance would not be prohibitively expensive. Making this request seems reasonable, since the money will be spent on raising your brother's children; furthermore, in the absence of such insurance, both his children and yours will suffer (I understand that if either your brother or his wife have any serious preexistent·medical conditions, insurance can easily become prohibitively expensive).

There is, of course, another issue involved. Does your husband truly not want to raise these children? If so, then you are really in a bind, because there is no way you can communicate such a response to your brother without causing genuine ill will. So, ask your husband to think about the following: In the event of such a tragedy occurring, would he really want to see these four children institutionalized? If he wouldn't, then he must be willing to accept the possibility, the remote possibility, of becoming your nephews' and nieces' legal guardians. At least you can be sure then of one thing: Your husband will be fervently praying for your brother and sister-in-law's good health.

Postscript: A reader reminded me that it would seem to be time for this woman and her husband to have a discussion about what provision they will make for their own children in case, God forbid, both of them die while their children are still young. The reader suggested that the wife ask the husband whom he would like to have take care of their children in such an eventuality, and maybe take advantage of this discussion to express the hope that these people will do so with greater enthusiasm than he has evinced toward his own brother-in-law's children.

※

Dear Joseph,

My father-in-law has forgotten my husband's birthday every year since we've been married. One year I couldn't stand it, so I called my father-in-law on the eve of my husband's birthday and reminded him. I tried to do it in a gentle way, but I sensed that my father-in-law was furious that I had "shamed" or "corrected" him. Our relationship has never been very warm or loving, and incidents like this just seem to add to the coolness between us.

My husband's fortieth birthday is coming up. I know that he will be terribly hurt if his father does not acknowledge it. On the one hand, I almost want the inevitable to happen and for my father-in-law to forget again and to be revealed as the self-involved, careless parent that I believe him to be. (Believe me, there is much more than forgotten birthdays to make me feel this way.) On the other hand, I want to protect my darling husband from any further pain. What should I do?

Unhappy Daughter-in-Law

Dear Unhappy Daughter-in-Law,

You don't mention whether you have a mother-in-law who can help you run interference, so I assume you don't. Therefore, the first thing I suggest is that you *not* speak again to your father-in-law about this matter. Clearly, the experience you mentioned was unpleasant for you, and caused an even further deterioration in the already negative relationship between you and him. Instead, I would suggest that you drop your father-in-law a note, worded as nicely as possible, saying something like this: "As you of course know, February 25 is Jim's birthday, and this year is a particularly significant one, his fortieth. I know how much his thoughts and feelings turn to his family at this time, as I trust yours turn to him. With warmest best wishes," and add on if you feel you can, "and with love."

Either your father-in-law will "come through" (success) or he won't; in which case he will be revealed as the overly self-involved person you believe him to be. But by avoiding speaking to him directly about your husband's birthday, you lessen the possibility of a defensive angry response, while your note simultaneously underscores how important a person he remains in his son's life.

I wish you a good resolution to this painful issue.

❦

Dear Joseph,

Oregon voters have approved an initiative that grants adopted children the right to full information about their births, including the names of parents who had been assured, when they gave the child up for adoption, that their identities would be kept secret. Whose rights should trump in such a case—a biological mother's right to privacy, or a child's right to know the answer to the most fundamental of questions: Who is my mommy?

Perplexed

Dear Perplexed,

Even before I address your broader query, my first instinct is to say that a child's mommy and daddy are the persons who have devoted their lives to raising her, to getting up in the middle of the night to calm her when she has nightmares or is sick, and who have supported her for many, many years. In addition to this mommy and daddy, an adopted child also has a biological connection to the woman who bore her and to the man by whom the woman conceived.

Human beings are naturally curious, and it makes sense that many adopted children want to know who gave birth to them. The child's claim to this knowledge strikes me as a strong one. One wants to be reassured that one comes from relatively normal people, and one wants to understand why this normal person gave her up for adoption. I suspect that such a meeting and reconciliation can be balm for the soul of the adopted child driven by such curiosity (we also know that it can sometimes be a disappointing, highly upsetting experience). Bear in mind, however, that *two-thirds* of adopted children, even those who live in states where it is easy to access information about one's birth parents, choose not to do so.

The situation in Oregon has an additional moral dimension. There was a time in America when having a child out of wedlock was almost universally considered to be disgraceful (as it is still felt to be among many Americans, although today more than a quarter of the babies in the United States are born to unmarried women). Therefore, the assurance to pregnant women that a child they put up for adoption would never learn the birth mother's identity was an important one. With such assurance, these women could go on with their lives knowing that they had provided their child with a two-parent home, and with the hope that they could now plan for their own futures without fearing that at some time the child would show up and her identity would have to be explained to their spouse and children.

Indeed, the dilemma as to "whose rights should trump" is a difficult one.

On balance, I believe that people who were given assurances of confidentiality have the right to expect those assurances to be honored. (On purely practical grounds, if these assurances are now violated, many people will justifiably never again trust promises made to them by government officials.) The adopted child might retort that her right to know a parent's identity is more pressing. But, in truth, the adopted child should realize that it was the very promise of confidentiality that might be the reason she is still alive. Had the pregnant woman not been given such an assurance, she might well have opted for an abortion, for even though abortions were then illegal, they were not uncommon.

However, I do see room for a compromise. Societal values have changed, and there is less shame today about giving birth out of wedlock (even among the more conservative elements within society, there tends to be a less negative attitude toward out-of-wedlock births). Many biological mothers who once insisted on privacy might now be open to knowing what has become of the child whom they carried for nine months. Therefore, instead of mandating that an adopted child's right to know is absolute, I suggest that state authorities transmit to the birth parent a request for the information the child wants, and let the mother make the choice as to whether or not to contact the child. (Only in an instance where medical information concerning the birth parent is truly necessary for the child's well-being should the state insist that the mother supply the information.)

A perfect solution? Hardly. But it probably will cause less pain than the alternative approaches that have been tried so far.

Dear Joseph,

My father is a nice man but dogmatically conservative. When my wife and I have dinner with my parents, he'll often go on and on about some issue. I generally disagree with him, and family dinners have become a bit uncomfortable. Lately, he's been denouncing abortion, and people who have abortions as baby killers. I happen to know that when my wife was in college she had an abortion, and my father's tirades are very painful to her. Should I tell my father about my wife's experience so that he'll stop being so insensitive? Or could that backfire and cause a permanent rift between them?

Abortion Secret

Dear Abortion Secret,

In courtrooms, witnesses are obliged to swear to tell "the truth, the whole truth, and nothing but the truth." Outside the courtroom, telling the whole truth can sometimes be unwise. Thus, I believe you are right to fear that if you inform your father about your wife's abortion, an act he regards as murder, you might well cause an irreparable rift between two of the most important people in your life. Therefore, I would suggest that you tell your father the truth—just not the whole truth—that you and your wife disagree strongly with his views on abortion. Indeed, you might tell him, for example, that you regard those who would insist on a raped woman being forced to bear the child of the man who violated and terrorized her as wrong. And that you feel similarly about those who would forbid abortion to a woman whose physical or emotional well-being was threatened by a pregnancy. Convey to your father that speaking about this issue makes family get-togethers unpleasant for you and your wife, and ask him whether he'd be willing to agree to disagree on this issue and not raise it. Make your conversation with him as loving as possible, and try to take as much sting out of your words as you can. Also, it might make sense to speak first with your mother. It's possible that she, not wishing to see family dinners become unpleasant (a pretty inevitable fate once an ideologue starts to dominate the discussion), can exert influence on your dad as well.

Unless your father is the sort of person who has a new cause he's espousing every week or two, I'd act on this matter quickly, before your wife starts to feel totally estranged from a man who will, God willing, be a part of your lives for many years. And remember to keep your anger in check, no matter how unpleasant the conversation with your father becomes. As you note in your letter's opening sentence, your "father is a nice man." In other words, you are having a disagreement with a nice man, not an enemy.

Postscript: In my response, I had noted that family dinners can become unpleasant when ideologues start to dominate the discussions, because for them, issues can become more important than people. One reader, whom I suspect is a bit of an ideologue, wrote in to argue that the father should "feel free to say anything he wishes in his own house. If your wife is sensitive on the subject, you can eat at home."

That a person is free to say anything he wants in his own house is inarguable—and pointless. Of course he's free to say what he likes, and of course the letter writer and his wife can eat at their own home. But while ideologues might think this is the preferred solution, most people who love both their parents and their spouse would prefer a solution that allows them to go on eating together, and to enjoy the experience.

Another writer chose to turn this subject into a feminist issue: "Maybe the guy should ask his wife if she feels like talking to the father. He seems to think she can't talk for herself."

That isn't the point, either. As a rule, if a family member is hurting one's spouse, it's the obligation of the partner who is more closely related to the offending party to speak to him or her. I would do so on my wife's behalf, and would expect her to do so on mine. Such behavior is popularly known as common sense, which, unfortunately, is not so common.

Dear Joseph,

We are taught to love and respect our parents. It seems odd to make people feel obligated to do this. What happens, as in my case, when I don't feel great love or respect for them?

Angry Child

Dear Angry Child,

Laws are intended to apply to the overwhelming majority of situations. Thus, when the Fifth Commandment legislated "Honor your father and mother," I believe it wished to offer a guideline that is almost but not always applicable. This is true of some of the other commandments as well. For example, I certainly believe in the Ninth Commandment's prohibition against offering false testimony. But had I lived in England two hundred years ago, at a time when people could be put to death even for minor acts of theft, I certainly hope that if I had witnessed such an act, I would have had the moral strength to offer false testimony and save the thief from death.

Regarding your question, I believe that there are parents who have acted so despicably as to free a child from the obligation to respect and love them. This would apply to parents who physically or sexually abused a child and also to instances of extreme verbal abuse or neglect. I believe it would also apply to a parent who enabled such abuse to occur (i.e., a parent who knew that his or her spouse was abusing their child and didn't intervene).

Otherwise, I think children have an innate obligation to offer respect and gratitude to their parents for conceiving and raising them. On occasion, people have challenged me on this, arguing that since they didn't ask to be born, they don't owe their parents anything for having brought them into the world.

This reminds me of an old Jewish folktale about a blind man and his deaf wife. One day, it was brought to their attention that a miracle-working doctor could cure both their ailments. The couple went to see the doctor, and sure enough he was able to make the deaf woman hear and the blind man see. The couple left the doctor's office, but within a few days realized that the cure was not making their lives easier. Now that the man could see, he noticed that his wife was very ugly, and found that his ardor for her had greatly diminished. Meanwhile, the woman realized that her husband had a foul mouth, and found that she was no longer attracted to him. Soon a bill came from the doctor's office, and the couple went there and told the physician that they weren't going to pay it; the operations had wreaked havoc with their formerly tranquil lives. The doctor said, "If that's how you feel about it, then don't pay." But he told the man, "You must then allow me to make you blind again, and your wife deaf." This, the couple was not willing to do, whereupon the doctor said, "Then it's clear that you prefer the improvements I have made in your life. So pay the bill."

A child who argues that he owes nothing to his parents because he didn't ask to be born is making a logical point only if he is willing to surrender his life. If, however, he enjoys living and wishes to go on doing so, then he must recognize that his parents, like the doctor in this story, did him a great favor.

A friend of mine always harbored angry feelings toward his parents. He felt that they never showed him much warmth, paid attention to what he said, or devoted time to him. Many years later, when he had his own children, his attitude toward his parents softened. He explained: "The mere fact that when I became an adult I had all my toes and fingers means that they were watching over me much more carefully than I ever thought."

Such vigilance and care deserves to be recognized. I urge adult children to telephone and visit their elderly parents often (particularly after one of them has become widowed), to make sure that their parents are aware of their gratitude, and to ensure that their parents are given the chance to establish a close relationship with their grandchildren. This is one of those commandments for which there is a clear payoff. Your children, after seeing you honor your parents, are far more likely to honor and take care of you when you grow old.

Finally, a thought about your last comment, that you don't feel respect for your parents. Some years ago, a man told me that he was in therapy and had been expressing to his therapist, over a period of many months, great bitterness toward his deceased father, an alcoholic workman who had treated him badly. The therapist told him that the rage he was experiencing was detrimental to him, and sent him home with the assignment that he come back with a list of three things about his father he could respect. The man followed the advice—the one thing I recall him telling me was that although his father was an alcoholic, he restricted his drinking to weekends and never missed a day of work because of it—and soon found that he felt better not only about his father, but about himself. I would advise you also to make a list of at least three things about your parents that you respect. If you can't come up with such a list, I suspect that even though you might have ground for grievance, you are being unfair to them.

✺

Dear Joseph,

I'm a twenty-one-year-old woman living in a one-room apartment in New York City with a fifteen-year-old cat. My father bought the cat for me when I was a child, but he never really wanted it, so when I took an apartment, he made me take the cat with me. Now the cat is old and sick (the veterinarian says there is not much he can do for her), and her odor is so bad that none of my friends will visit my apartment. Needless to say, this is terrible for my social life. Also, the constant stench from the cat is making me sick, and her loud meowing at night often makes it hard for me to sleep. Would it be immoral for me to put the cat to sleep?

Sleepless in New York

Dear Sleepless in New York,

For those who believe there is no real difference between human and animal life—because all life is equally holy—the answer is obvious: You must keep the cat alive and bear with the consequences. After all, you wouldn't kill a human being because her smell was adversely affecting your social life.

For those who believe that animal life is of little value, the answer is equally clear: When an animal becomes inconvenient, eliminate the inconvenience.

My view falls in between. I believe that animal life has value, but that it's less than that of human life. Thus, I eat meat (I say this without pride; I would be a better person if I didn't). But I also believe that people develop special relationships with their pets and that these relationships impose upon them some distinct obligations. Thus, I believe that people are morally required to have their pets treated by veterinarians (not just to get the shots required by state law) to cure illnesses, and to minimize the chances of an animal becoming sick and suffering pain. But what if a person does not have the money to go to a vet? Then, I would argue, he or she has no moral right to own a pet.

During my childhood, we never had pets in our house, so I grew up without a special affection for animals. But my wife has a great love of animals, my children are crazy about our two cats, and I've mellowed over the years.

Two years ago, one of our cats, Snowbell, became sick with diabetes. We learned how to administer insulin shots to her. Even with her blood sugar better regulated, Snowbell started to deteriorate and develop other illnesses. My wife eventually was feeding the cat intravenously. Ultimately, Snowbell lost two-thirds of her weight, and we were ready to put her to sleep; only when we took her to the vet to do so, Snowbell looked at us with such alertness in her eyes that we felt we couldn't go ahead. We took the cat home, until it became apparent that her suffering was so great that it was time to put her to sleep.

Our reaction was perhaps on the extreme side, in terms of both the money and time we—and particularly my wife—were willing to expend. But our reaction need not be binding on you. For one thing, the fact that you live in a tiny apartment, and that it constantly smells horrible, is a real consideration. When I go into a very bad-smelling environment I begin to gag, and the thought of having to live in such an environment all the time is horrifying. Also cause for real concern is the fact that keeping alive a sickly fifteen-year-old cat means that people won't visit your home and that you have trouble sleeping at night.

I therefore propose that you revisit your vet and find out if there is anything you can do to help the cat and to stop the smell. Second, go on the Internet and find out if there are services that will take in old, sickly cats (I'm taking it for granted that no one will want to adopt such a cat). If there are, you should be willing to pay a reasonable amount so that your cat can have a decent end to her life.

If indeed there is nothing the vet can do and you can find no such services, then I don't believe it is immoral to put this animal to sleep. When I told my wife what I was planning to answer, she disagreed, arguing that it is spiritually wrong to put the animal to sleep, unless it is clearly suffering greatly. I understand her view, but in my opinion, constant and extreme bad odor in one's house, an inability to bring over friends, and nights of sleeplessness constitute significant suffering on your part, and would justify putting your unfortunate cat to sleep—but only after you have checked out these two other alternatives.

※

Dear Joseph,

My mother recently passed on. I had been living with her for two years, taking care of her. Her house is to go up for sale, and I may have to get an apartment. She put in her will that her dog, who is old and somewhat sickly, should be put down. But the dog still plays with us and my son's younger dog, as well as with my son and his three children. I want to follow my mother's wishes, but don't agree that the dog should be killed. [I've] even thought it has shown grief since her illness first began. Can you help me?

Animal Lover

Dear Animal Lover,

I assume that your mother's request that the dog be put to death was motivated by her love for it. Because the animal is old and somewhat sickly, she perhaps feared that it would not be well cared for, and therefore that the most merciful thing would be to kill it.

But you and your son's family are willing to

bestow loving attention on this dog. I find it hard to imagine that had your mother envisioned that such care would be provided she still would have wanted to see her beloved pet killed. Therefore, I don't believe you should follow this provision of your mother's will. To kill an animal that still has some quality of life, that does not impose undue hardships on those who are taking care of it, and that is being provided with loving care strikes me as wrong.

TWO

Children

Dear Joseph,

I am a family educator at an Atlanta private school, and also work with professional development of preschool teachers. In both arenas, I have spent a lot of time exploring core values. Last week, at a conference for early-childhood educators, I went to a workshop on values led by a professor who has written many books on the subject. She proudly displayed a list of around 150 values that were compiled from hundreds of students and clients (e.g., including happiness, which she taught was a value rather than a consequence of leading a meaningful life). During the question-and-answer period, I asked the professor, "Do you ever use the words 'right' and 'wrong'?" She answered by saying that she usually rephrases with a question of "What is a better way of handling it?" After the professor answered my question, she said,

"Now, you may think it is important to use the words 'right' and 'wrong.' I'm interested in knowing why you think it is so important." Well, she caught me off guard. I want to be able to answer why I'm bothered by her fluid definitions. Can you help me?

A Believer in Right and Wrong

Dear Believer in Right and Wrong,

In my view, it's important that children learn at a young age that there are certain things that are right and certain things that are wrong. It is quite remarkable how, in the absence of such knowledge, people can end up rationalizing pretty much any evil, just as Lenin is reputed to have justified the murders of anti-Communists with the infamous statement "You can't make an omelet without breaking eggs." I use the word *wrong*, therefore, to be moral and accurate. There simply are things that are wrong, and they should be labeled as such.

I suspect that your disagreement with this professor revolves around an even more fundamental disagreement, one about human nature. If human beings were born naturally good, as I assume this professor believes, it would indeed be sufficient to simply ask, "How would you handle it?" However, I am more inclined to accept the Bible's observation on human nature: "The tendency of man's heart is towards evil from his youth" (Genesis 8:21). This verse doesn't mean that human beings are born evil or in a state of sin. What Genesis is suggesting is that evil and selfishness are more natural to human beings than goodness and altruism. As Dennis Prager once pointed out, "If children were born naturally good, you'd walk into a house and hear a mother yelling at her three-year-old son, 'Johnny, when are you going to stop being so selfless and giving all your toys away to the other children in the neighborhood?'" Instead, children have to be taught goodness and generosity; for most, it doesn't come naturally.

A friend of mine lectured on more than a dozen occasions before classes of teenagers, and asked them what they thought about shoplifting. He was discomfited to learn that more than half said that they would shoplift if they knew they wouldn't be caught. The teens defended their view with arguments such as "The stores overcharge for their products, so when I take something, it's not really stealing; I'm just getting back some of what I've been overcharged." (As Freud is reputed to have said, "When it comes to self-deception, every man is a genius.") In other words, because these young people didn't want to see themselves as thieves, which shoplifters are, they imagined themselves as Robin Hoods, stealing from the rich store owners and giving to the poor—in this case, themselves.

Equally disappointing were the responses offered by many of the teenagers who said they wouldn't shoplift. Having been raised in a society that is reluctant to use terms like *right* and *wrong*, they explained their refusal to shoplift with statements such as "I wouldn't feel comfortable doing that, but I wouldn't condemn someone who did."

Given that we have just left a century in which humankind experienced, among other horrors, the Holocaust, the Gulag Archipelago, and mass murders in China, Cambodia, and Rwanda, I would turn the question back to your professor: "Why are you so uncomfortable calling some acts 'right' and some 'wrong'?"

In short, acts such as shoplifting are wrong no matter how one chooses to "handle it" when one talks about it. The same holds for another act that is common in schools (and that damages many young people's lives): humiliating a classmate by labeling him or her with a painful nickname. Children should be taught that if they call a child by an offensive nickname, they're doing something wrong.

Finally, I presume that even this professor would deem it *wrong,* even evil, for a pedophile to try to get a job in a school. And if she were the principal, I don't think she would want to have a long conversation with the pedophile about how he would handle it.

G. K. Chesterton wisely reminds us that "there is something to be said for every error, but whatever may be said for it, the most important thing to be said about it is that it is erroneous."

Postscript: Readers had a broad range of reactions. One correspondent, perhaps building upon the logic of the professor at the conference, expressed a view that even the professor might have found discomfiting: "There is no such thing as right. There is no such thing as wrong. There is only what you choose for yourself."

This comment reminded me of something I had read years ago in Oliver Martin's *Two Educators:* " 'Bad' people like Hitler and Goering simply carried out more or less consistently many of the ideas long held by respectable 'good' people. . . . How do good people deny morality? In many ways:

" 'I believe in morals but all morals are relative.'

" 'I have my own private moral code.'

" 'Morals are entirely a matter of opinion.'

" 'There are no absolutes in morals that can rationally be discovered.' "

Martin concluded that "a Hitler or Mussolini could accept every one of these statements."

On the other hand, one reader shared with me a stunning insight as to why articulating moral values is so important: "A generation of children raised in a morally neutral environment will yield a society where no truths can be held as self-evident."

Dear Joseph,

I have a friend who clearly favors one of her two young sons over the other. When the older child acts badly, she finds a million excuses to justify his behavior. But if the younger one does something the slightest bit wrong, she comes down on him like a "ton of bricks" (she doesn't hit him, but she's verbally very harsh). I want to say something to her, yet I'm very uncomfortable at the thought of doing so. She's a dear friend, and I don't want to lose her friendship.

Worried and Uncomfortable

Dear Worried and Uncomfortable,

Whenever someone considers criticizing another person, I suggest that she first ask herself: "Am I looking forward to offering this criticism, or would I give anything not to?"

If you're looking forward to offering criticism, don't. Your motives are probably insincere (perhaps even a little hostile), and the other person is likely to become defensive, and not be influenced by your words.

Because you're apparently unhappy to be in this situation, your motives seem good. And while I don't envy you, it also seems clear that the right thing to do is to speak with your friend. Children need advocates. When the natural advocate, the child's parent, can't be trusted to be fair, the responsibility shifts to others.

In speaking to your friend, your words are more likely to be effective if you:

- *Make it clear that you care deeply for her.* It is easier for a person to hear criticism and change her behavior when criticism is delivered lovingly (hence, my suggestion to keep one's mouth shut when one is looking forward to offering the criticism). Also, if your friend feels that you hold her in esteem, she will be more likely to try to act in a manner that will cause you to continue respecting and liking her.

- *Mention to her very specific instances in which you witnessed how she treated one child unfairly.* If you only offer a general critique, she will probably deny your accusation; likewise, if you cite only one instance. It's harder to deny the truth when it is illustrated by several concrete examples.

If it becomes clear that your friend feels some ambivalence about the child whom she's treating unfairly, as I suspect it will, I would urge you to urge *her* to seek professional help. (You don't mention whether or not the woman is married, but there is a good chance that her feelings toward this child are tied to her feelings toward the child's father. In my experience, when a couple gets along harmoniously, and one of their children has a trait that reminds one parent of the other, that trait endears the child to the parent. But when a couple is in conflict, and there's real anger between them, it is precisely those traits of the child that remind the parent of his or her spouse [or ex-spouse], that most get on a parent's nerves.)

Parents playing favorites among their children is a particularly troublesome issue. A young child is entitled to unconditional love, which is exactly what an unfavored child does not receive. Is there a greater emotional disadvantage than growing up with the feeling that even your parent doesn't love you?

Parental favoritism can also imperil the whole family structure. Thus, the Bible (in Genesis, chapter 37) relates how Jacob loved Joseph more than his other sons and, like the woman about whom you're writing, made no effort to disguise his favoritism. He freed Joseph from the chores his other sons were expected to perform, and provided him with more beautiful clothing.

Jacob's undisguised favoritism was an important, probably the most important, factor in causing his other sons to hate Joseph and to sell him into slavery. Indeed, this story reminds us that when parental love cannot be taken for granted, sibling love also becomes endangered. If you want children to grow up loving and appreciating one another, they need to feel that they are not competing for a finite supply of parental love.

I know you're uncomfortable with what you must do, and I would be, too. But if you can influence this mother to change her behavior, or to seek professional help, you will have helped spare a vulnerable boy from unnecessary suffering. What a wonderful opportunity to do something that can permanently affect another person's life for the better.

※

Dear Joseph,

My three-year-old and five-year-old take delight in squashing ants on the sidewalk. I've tried to tell them that it's bad to kill living things, but they've seen me swat bees and spiders in the house, so I feel hypocritical. How can I explain the difference to them?

Guilty Hypocrite

Dear Guilty Hypocrite,

Guess what. You're not a guilty hypocrite. When you kill a bee in your home, there is a reason for you to do so—the insect is somewhat dangerous, and you have a right to protect yourself and your family. But when your children squash ants on the sidewalk, there is no reason for them to do so; the ants pose no danger and aren't bothering them. You would, however, be a hypocrite if you went out into a forest to an area containing many bees, just for the pleasure of killing them.

I heard a story told about the late Rabbi Israel Spira, a Holocaust survivor, who had seen in his lifetime the worst of which human beings are capable, and who had become, perhaps in consequence, exceedingly careful not to cause any needless suffering to human beings or animals. Once, when he saw one of his grandchildren purposely step on an ant, he said to him, "Oh, how sad! The ants were marching joyfully to a wedding, and now you've killed the groom."

The young boy felt bad and deeply regretted what he had done. By personalizing the insects, as the rabbi did, you may similarly motivate your two young children to feel more compassion for all living creatures.

As for killing spiders and other scary-but-not-dangerous insects, wouldn't it be better to try to pick them up on a newspaper or large piece of paper and carry them outside? There's no reason to kill insects when there is no need to do so, and there are relatively easy alternatives available. If your children see you act in this manner (i.e., swatting dangerous insects or genuinely bothersome ones such as mosquitoes, but trying to avoid killing nondangerous ones), they might change their own behavior.

But what if they don't? Is this an issue you should be concerned about? I believe you should, particularly if such behavior persists over the coming years. It is sadistic to kill a living creature just for pleasure; the mere fact that someone enjoys doing that—particularly as he gets older—is cause for concern. I know a woman who was dating a man who told her that, as a child, he used to cut insects in half for fun. She married him, and when he became angry at her, he beat her. True, there may not be a correlation, but if one of my daughters were dating someone who had spent his childhood killing insects for pleasure, I'd worry.

Your children are now very young, so there's certainly no cause for you to panic. But this is an issue that must be addressed. Whatever a person's age, there is one thing human beings are not in need of, and that is to get more in touch with their sadistic inclinations.

A final thought: I have no idea whether your family is religious, but if it is, it might be worthwhile as your children get older to teach them that the Bible places great emphasis on human beings treating animals in a kind manner. For example, Deuteronomy 25:4 states, "You shall not muzzle an ox while it is threshing," because it is cruel to muzzle an animal that is working in the presence of food; rather, you must let the animal eat where it is working. Deuteronomy 22:10 forbids harnessing two animals of unequal strength (for instance, an ox and a donkey) in a field, for one will suffer frustration, the other strain. Deuteronomy 22:6 rules that if a person comes across a nest of birds, he or she cannot take the mother bird along with the young, but must send the mother away to spare her feelings. Concerning the rationale for this law, the great medieval Jewish philosopher Moses Maimonides wrote that "the pain of the animals under such circumstances is very great."

Dear Joseph,

My ten-year-old daughter, along with one other girl in her class, were the only ones not invited to a birthday party for a girl at school. The birthday girl has been teased by many of those invited to the party because she is overweight. By contrast, my daughter has been nice to her, inviting her to sleepovers and parties. We have often driven her, along with the other girl not invited, to gymnastics classes, and had her stay at our house when her parents arrived home late from work. Now, in return, my daughter has been snubbed. As a parent, I am angry. My daughter, who is obviously a better person than I, is somewhat hurt, but says, "Well, maybe we just didn't get the invitation in the mail." I doubt that. My first, and still my preferred, response to the situation is to call the parents and demand a reason. What would you do?

Mama Lioness

Dear Mama Lioness,

Your instinct to speak to the parents is the right one. Indeed, I believe you have an ethical obligation both to your daughter and to the offending parents to make such a call.

You owe it to your daughter because it's important for her to know that her parents take her pain and embarrassment seriously. I also think it's worth speaking to your daughter's class teacher and the school principal, particularly if your daughter attends a private school. At the school my children attend, the principal has established a policy that while a child can invite three or four classmates to a small party, once she invites more, she is obligated to invite the entire class (that is, a girl must invite all the girls; a boy must invite all the boys). This principal has wisely intuited that to leave out a few children is so unkind and humiliating that it must be forbidden. I emphasize that I am speaking about a private school because I simply don't know if it would be permitted at a public school for a principal or teacher to establish such a policy.

As regards the offending parents, there are two reasons you should speak to them. First, given that your daughter and your family have gone out of your way to be hospitable and gracious to this girl, there is at least a chance that an invitation was lost in the mail. Admittedly, the possibility of this having happened is small, particularly since this other girl also received no invitation (and for all the griping one hears about the post office, it's very unlikely that they would lose two invitations).

Second, assuming that the girl and her parents did purposely exclude your daughter, then it is important that you communicate to them your daughter's hurt. The reason I suggest that you emphasize the hurt your daughter experienced rather than the annoyance you justifiably feel is that annoyance is more apt to trigger an unsympathetic, defensive response, while pain is more likely to cause people to reconsider what they have done. I would also ask the parents why your daughter wasn't invited. If they say something like "My daughter didn't want your daughter at the party because she doesn't like her," I would ask them if they think it's worth acceding to their daughter's wishes in such a case. Wouldn't it be better for the two girls to try to work out whatever differences they have rather than to act in a manner that is likely to create a permanent barrier of hurt and ill will?

As the father of young children, I know how much I suffer when they're hurt. And it is a pain that lingers. An elderly woman I know, a highly ethical person, told me that when her daughter was in the second grade, she and two other girls were not invited to another child's party. It was a fancy event, and the next day many of the other girls came to school with beautiful dolls that had been given to them as party favors. Only when this woman picked up her daughter at school and saw the other girls playing with the dolls did she realize what had happened. Though shocked, she was too shy ever to confront the mother. And yet she confessed to me that more than thirty years later when she heard that the mother who had given the party, a woman who was known to be quite nice and philanthropic, had died, the first thought that went through her head was that this woman had not invited her daughter to that second-grade party.

An extreme reaction? Perhaps, but I tell this story not for your benefit, but for the benefit of those parents who allow their children to exclude some children from their parties. Such parents should be aware that doing so can cause great pain, and may unleash an anger against you much greater than you can ever imagine.

Postscript: A letter that a reader sent me illustrates the lingering hurt such an experience can inflict, although her story has a partly happy ending:

"I still remember an incident in middle school, when a popular student and an unpopular student gave a party on the same day. Almost all of the students went to the 'unpopular' party, stayed just long enough to collect party favors, then got up and left to go to the more popular party. I can still remember the look on the birthday girl's face when forty kids got up and left her party after half an hour. I can't imagine parents who would allow their children to act so hurtfully.

"If there is a happy ending to the story, it's that I still see a few of the five or six kids who stayed. All of them grew up to be caring and happy adults, probably better people than the ones that acted so selfishly. But that wasn't much consolation at the time."

Dear Joseph,

My daughter, who's in the eighth grade, is applying to high schools. She's on the wild side, and the kind of kid who is very—I suppose overly—influenced by her environment. There is one school that I think can exert a very positive influence on her, but based on her current grades, she won't get in. That is, unless . . . You see, I am pretty prominent in my community and have the connections to get her admitted. My wife insists that I do everything I can to get her in. But I'm conflicted. The school is very selective, which means that if my daughter gets in, some other kid probably won't. Is it wrong to use my connections to get my daughter admitted?

Conflicted

Dear Conflicted,

Several years ago, a friend of mine confronted a case remarkably similar to yours. His son applied to a school, and the principal, a dear friend, told him that he didn't think the boy, whose problems were similar to those of your daughter, was an appropriate candidate for the school. It soon came out, however, that because of their long-standing friendship, the principal would admit the boy if the father insisted. The father did insist, the boy was admitted, and within the year his bad grades and involvement with drugs forced the parents to withdraw him.

Seeing how badly things had turned out, I asked the father whether he regretted having intervened so forcefully to get his son admitted. He told me that he had no regrets: "If I hadn't gotten him in, and he had gone to another school, it's very likely he would also have done badly and ended up on drugs. And then, I would have tortured myself, thinking, 'Oh, if I'd only gotten him into that other school, then everything would have worked out.'"

I believe that you have the obligation to find the school that will best meet your daughter's needs. But you also must make sure that that is the only criterion you are using, that you want her in this school because it will best address her needs, and not because of a desire on your part to have her attend a prestigious school.

If this school is right for her, then do what you can to get her admitted, within the bounds of the law (e.g., don't try to bribe anyone, though admittedly some parents find a legal way to do so by making it known that they are considering making a large contribution to the school).

If you don't use your connections on your daughter's behalf, are you going to be comfortable five or ten years from now telling her that you could have gotten her into this school, only you chose not to do so?

I recognize that the position I am advocating is morally problematic, and in a perfect world, the use of personal influence would be wrong. But as my friend J. J. Goldberg, editor of the *Forward*, said when I discussed with him the dilemma raised in your letter, "It's like the issue of nuclear disarmament. Why would one nation ever be so foolish as to be the first to disarm without guarantees that other nations were doing so as well?" In other words, if you refuse to use connections for your child in a world where other parents are using connections for their children, you're doing your child a disservice, just as a nation's leader does a disservice to his people's security by disarming at a time when other nations are not doing so.

In short, parents have special responsibilities to, and for, their children. If this school can help shape and greatly enrich the rest of your daughter's life, I would suggest that you do what you can to get her in.

Dear Joseph,

My seventeen-year-old daughter is pregnant and won't be marrying the baby's father. Since she is keeping the child, she would like to have a baby shower. My problem is how do I show love for the sinner but not for the sin? I feel that if I host this party, I will be condoning her actions. I don't know where to turn for guidance. What should I do?

Distraught Mother

Dear Distraught Mother,

While I don't find the language of sin—which seems to put the stress primarily on the act of premarital sex—to be helpful in this case, I understand your unhappiness. It is, in my view, unfair to a baby to intentionally bring him into the world without both a mommy and a daddy to care for and love him. In addition, your daughter's young age virtually guarantees that either she will have to give up her education prematurely, or that you, as the grandmother, will end up raising the child and paying for the baby's expenses.

Therefore, given that you feel that it's morally wrong for your daughter to have gotten pregnant in these circumstances, I understand your desire not to host a baby shower. I, therefore, don't believe that you are responsible or obligated to do so. Your daughter is the one who became pregnant. If she wishes to have a baby shower, let her host it (obviously, not at your home) or let her get a friend to do it.

Let me suggest, however, an alternative. Wait

until after the birth of the baby and, if you then feel so inclined (which you might, once you see a tangible, adorable child), give a party in the baby's honor. While hosting a baby shower for your pregnant daughter does not feel right to you and may send her the wrong message, a celebration after the baby is born comes across as a celebration of the life of this child; and every baby, whether born in or out of wedlock, deserves to have his or her life celebrated.

꙰

Dear Joseph,

I am a single parent of two girls. Going to school each morning has become an absolute nightmare. My girls, who are six and seven, already are so fashion-conscious that I'm beginning to hate dressing them. Each morning, they're in tears and bad temper because of their fear of being teased about the clothes I can afford to dress them in. I want to know if there are any parents out there who feel the same way, and wonder if you have any ideas about what can be done about this problem.

Mother of Two Unhappy Daughters

Dear Mother of Two Unhappy Daughters,

When you mentioned that your daughters were teased in school because of their clothes, I immediately recalled a sad article I read several years ago in the *New York Times* (October 14, 1998, page 1). The paper profiled a girl named Wendy, who lived with her family in a trailer park and who attended a school largely made up of children from affluent homes. Her peers repeatedly made Wendy feel miserable because her clothing was far less attractive than theirs.

Once, she saw a girl in a beautiful new shirt and asked her where she had bought it. The girl laughed, and said, "Why would you want to know?" Wendy confided to the reporter that she knew the shirt was out of her price range, but she just wanted to be part of the small talk. Another time, a classmate teased Wendy about her mismatched clothes, then went on to make fun of her humble home. When the boy wouldn't stop, Wendy kicked him in the shins. When he complained to the school authorities, she was placed on suspension.

While I'm sure your daughters are encountering teasing much less severe than this, as I read your letter I was thinking that there is, of course, something that can be done about this problem: school uniforms. Such a requirement wouldn't mean that a child has to wear the same outfit each day, which children rightly regard as boring. Rather, students could have a choice among three or four permissible outfits to be worn.

The greatest benefit of uniforms is moral. Students whose parents lack the means to buy them the kind of clothes worn by their wealthier peers would be spared embarrassment. That your children go to school in fear of being mocked because of their clothes is outrageous. That you, a single mother, have to spend far more on clothes for your children than you probably can afford is also outrageous.

I believe that any school with a student body from widely dissimilar economic backgrounds is obliged to prevent students from being humiliated because they can't afford the style of clothes the more affluent students can. While it's true that life is unfair, the time to learn this unhappy truth should not be the first and second grades, or at any point in elementary school.

Uniforms, particularly for girls, will have not only moral benefits, but psychological ones as well. While my experience is that young boys usually couldn't care less about what they or their classmates are wearing, girls care a lot about such matters, and spend way too much time worrying about their clothes. As it is, females in our country derive too much of their sense of self-worth from how attractive they feel. Undue attention to clothes only furthers this focus on the physical.

I am interested in hearing opposing views (which undoubtedly I will hear from my ten- and twelve-year-old daughters), but it seems obvious to me that for moral, psychological, and intellectual reasons, all children, but particularly girls, will flourish more in schools that require uniforms.

Postscript: In line with Robert Burns's poetic truism "The best laid schemes o' mice an' men / Gang aft agley," a reader who attended a high school that required uniforms informed me that such a system did not yield quite the happy solution I thought it would: "It in no way bridged the gap between rich and poor or reduced undue care about clothing. The problem merely became more subtle—you could still find the wealthy kids by looking for the little Polo horse on their shirts or the Gucci loafers or the Coach bags."

Most other readers who wrote in, however, supported my suggestion. As a reader from "Down Under" put it: "I've lived most all my life in Australia. Here school uniforms are the norm, for both private and state schools. I am so glad that, during those difficult years, I at least did not have to worry about what people would make of what I wore between 9 A.M. and 3 P.M. five days a week."

Dear Joseph,

I had a very unsettling experience recently. I was at an informal affair at a friend's house, one at which both adults and children were present. A little girl, she must have been about three or four, was running around, and she knocked into a table and caused some food and drinks to spill. Her father came over to her, and got down on his knees. I was the only adult nearby, and I was impressed. I figured he was trying to connect with his daughter on her eye level. Only I was shocked by what he then said: "What you did was very stupid. I want you to say to me, 'Daddy, I am very stupid.'" Sure enough, the little girl, intimidated by her father, repeated the words just as he had told her. I was in shock, and said nothing. What should I have done?

Angry and Ashamed

Dear Angry and Ashamed,

You have a right to be both angry and ashamed. When I read your letter, I winced, and afterward I felt overcome with pain. How could any father force a child to so humiliate herself, and start her on the path to developing a lifelong miserable self-image?

I suspect your instinct must be the one I had, to wish that I could find a way to force this cruel fool to say the very words he was forcing his daughter to say: "I am very stupid." Indeed, those words would be gentler than the real words that might better apply: "I am acting very meanly."

Obviously, if you had any reason to believe your words would make an impact, the best thing would have been to approach the man and, in as noncon-frontational a manner as possible, say to him, "I'm sure you don't intend it, but forcing your daughter to make such a statement will have a very detrimental effect on her, and make her feel that she is a very unworthy person."

However, from your letter, I get the impression that you didn't know the man at all and therefore felt uncomfortable getting involved. Also, it's possible that you feared that any words you might say to such an insensitive person would antagonize him, and that after you went away he would take out his anger on his defenseless child.

If that is the reason you were quiet, here are some other thoughts about what you could do. If someone was present at the event who knew the man better than you, you might seek out that person, and tell him precisely what you witnessed and ask him if he could speak to the child's father. Alternatively, you could find out if the man's wife was present. If so, tell her what you witnessed. Or, let's assume for a moment the man was divorced, an assumption that might well be true, since it's hard to imagine an adult woman choosing to live with so verbally cruel a spouse. If so, you could make an effort to find out the ex-wife's name and phone number and call and tell her what you had witnessed, remaining anonymous if you feel too nervous to become more directly involved. Having this information might be useful to the woman if she were involved in any litigation trying to limit the father's visitation rights with his daughter.

Another possibility: When you heard the daughter saying, "Daddy, I am very stupid," you could have started talking to the girl in a manner that would have made it seem that you had not heard her father force her to say these words, but that you assumed that she had said these words on her own. Then, you could have said something along the lines of "Oh, don't say such a thing. I'm sure it makes your daddy feel so sad to hear his lovely little daughter call herself stupid. You're not stupid just because you knocked over some food or spilled a drink. I've done that plenty of times, and I'm not stupid. And I bet your daddy's done it, too, at least once." And then you could have turned to the father and asked him, "Haven't you?"

That way, one of two things might have happened. The man might have realized how excessively he had responded, be ashamed of what he had done, and acted differently. Alternatively, even if you didn't succeed in modifying the father's behavior, the little girl might have remembered that there was another adult present who didn't think it right that her father made her call herself stupid. At least that could help her maintain better self-esteem while she continued to live in a verbally abusive household.

Postscript: Several responses to this column came from victims of abuse, and were as sad as the letter to which I was responding. The most painful came from a reader who wrote, "As an abused daughter, sir, everything you suggested would have been impossible to attempt." Another reader also felt that talking to a person capable of such verbal abuse would have been an exercise in futility, and possibly worse: "Very good suggestions, but not likely to do anything but get the girl into more trouble at another time. My stepfather always called me 'Stupid' and my brother 'Sissy.' The best advice in my opinion: Strike up a conversation with the girl privately and let her know she is not stupid. When you have someone like that in your life, a few kind words from a stranger can stick with you."

One reader, however, challenged the moral correctness of ever publicly confronting such a parent: "While I completely agree that this is an incorrect way to discipline a child, I do not feel that it is anyone's responsibility to criticize publicly how a parent disciplines their own child." While I had not said anything about criticizing the offending parent in public, I assume what the writer meant was that parents should not be criticized for how they discipline their child in public. This e-mail in turn provoked this insightful response: "You must remember that emotionally abused children grow up to become emotionally disturbed adults . . . and emotionally disturbed adults become everyone's problem."

The writer's point, suggesting that abusive parents are enemies not only of the children they abuse but potentially of all of us, is profound. Recently, I read Jonathan Glover's *Humanity: A Moral History of the Twentieth Century.* One of the things that jumped out at me was how harshly strict, and often abusive, childhood was for the future leaders of Nazi Germany. For example, Adolf Hitler's father, Alois, forbade his children to speak in his presence unless instructed to do so. He didn't call his son by his name, Adolf, but would put two fingers in his mouth and whistle for him in the same way he whistled for his dog. Hitler's half brother recalled Alois's "very violent temper," which often led him to beat his children, and sometimes his wife, and hit his dog so hard that the animal urinated on the floor. Rudolf Hoess, the future commandant of Auschwitz, recalled how his father "hauled me out of bed one night because I had left the saddle-cloth lying in the garden instead of hanging it in the barn to dry, as he had told me to do." How long is the path from this type of harsh, mean-spirited upbringing to Hitler's later vision: "I want the young to be violent, domineering, undismayed, cruel. The young must be all these things. They must be able to bear pain. There must be no thing weak or gentle about them. The free, splendid beast of prey must once again flash from their eyes." Glover cites the striking claim of Alice Miller, author of *For Your Own Good: Hidden Cruelty in Child-Rearing and the Roots of Violence*, that she could not find, among all the leaders of Nazi Germany, one who did not have a rigid, overly strict upbringing. As Glover concludes, "[H]ow much the world owes to the childhood humiliation of Hitler by his father cannot be known for sure. It is not a universal truth that those to whom evil is done do evil in return, but it is true often enough, and Hitler is one instance."

In short, abusive parents raise children who are disproportionately likely to inflict abuse on others. That is just one additional reason why such abuse should concern the general society.

Because so much abuse takes place in private, it is, to a large extent, an insoluble social problem. George Bernard Shaw wrote a century ago (in *Everybody's Political What's What*), "Parentage is a very important profession, but no test of fitness for it is ever imposed in the interest of the children." Or as my friend Max Prager used to point out, in New York you have to have a license to sell bagels, while anybody with a sexual organ is permitted to have children.

Dear Joseph,

My son's Little League baseball coach plays his own kid at first base, even though my ten-year-old son is a more talented first baseman. I know this father's a volunteer and gives a lot of his time, but shouldn't he play the kids on the basis of skill, not nepotism?

Can't-Get-to-First-Base

Dear Can't-Get-to-First-Base,

Of course you're right; of course a coach should play the children on the basis of skill and not nepotism. But the truth is that even the best-intentioned people can act unwisely and unfairly when their own emotions are involved. The coach, who is also a father, is functioning in two roles. As a father, he has an obligation to show special concern for his own son; as a coach, he should treat all his players equally.

Clearly, it would be better if the team's coach were not also the father of one of the players. On the other hand, the Little League relies on volunteers to serve as coaches, and without fathers in that role, the Little League probably would have a great shortage of coaches.

I suggest the following: Go to the coach with another father and express your concern. Suggest that the decision about "Who's on first?"—and that decision alone—should be made by a father who is unrelated to any of the possible first basemen. The coach is probably not going to take kindly to this suggestion. And it's possible that, if an "outsider" decides to bench his son and substitute another player, the coach might conclude that he no longer wishes to volunteer his services. Would you then be ready to step in?

If you aren't, I'm not blaming you. I'm just being

realistic. Also, while I understand your frustration, imagine the following: You take over as coach, put your son in at first, and then, a month from now, a kid shows up at practice, whose abilities a lot of other people seem to think are superior to your son's. How readily would you come to that conclusion and substitute that player for your son? In other words, I'm not saying your critique of the coach is incorrect; rather, I'm just trying to get you to be a little more sympathetic to his dilemma.

Finally, if your attempt at arbitration with the coach fails, what then? You can try to find a new team for your son, try to get a new coach appointed (though this, you can be sure, is likely to lead to terrible acrimony), or maybe try to see if your son has aptitude at another position. Can you imagine if it turns out that he's a great third baseman or left fielder? Good luck.

Dear Joseph,

My son is filling out his college applications and has several essays to write. He isn't the greatest writer, and I've been doing some fairly heavy editing (okay, rewriting) on his work. I'm feeling a little guilty, but it's a very competitive world today for kids. I even know parents who shell out a lot of money for experts to work with teenagers on their essays. If everyone else gets help and my son gets none, I'm afraid he won't get accepted anywhere.

Ghostwriter

Dear Ghostwriter,

Your question is an important one, and I find that I can't come up with a definitive response. On the one hand, what you are doing is a kind of cheating. And what if many kids at your son's school were cheating on tests, and, by refusing to do so, your son was jeopardizing his prospects for getting into a good college? Would you then advocate that he cheat? I would hope not.

Some years ago, Dennis Prager made a documentary, *For Goodness Sake!*, in which he showed a mother defending her son's cheating with arguments remarkably similar to yours: It's very competitive out there, and, if he doesn't cheat, he won't get in to good schools; everybody else does it. The documentary cuts to a scene of this same woman being wheeled into surgery. With a frightened look on her face, she asks the doctor, "You're very confident about the procedure you're performing, aren't you?" And the doctor responds, "I don't know, lady. I cheated my way through medical school."

Therefore, my first response is that writing your son's essay for him is wrong. But what about minor editing? That would seem to me to be okay, since if schools truly expected students to submit work done by them and them alone, they would do the following: Have a large number of colleges decide on certain similar essay questions, and then have those questions responded to by students sitting in a classroom with a proctor present. This would guarantee that the work submitted by the students was done without help.

I spoke about the dilemma raised in your letter with an independent college counselor, a woman who helps high-school students with their applications to Ivy League and other high-ranking schools. She acknowledged the difficulty in formulating a hard-and-fast rule as to what parents should and shouldn't do in helping their children with college essays, but she did affirm the importance of "drawing a line between helping your child and substituting your abilities for his." Doing so is unfair both to the college that is assessing your child's application and to your child himself. By presenting your child as a far better writer than he is, you put him at risk of being exposed as a fraud later on. Thus, it's better to prod your child and awaken his interest in the subject of the essay, have him write down his (not your) ideas, and then limit your involvement to relatively minor grammatical and stylistic improvements.

This college counselor also suggested that to somewhat even the playing field for a child with few resources (and to assuage your guilt), you could volunteer to help a student who lacks access to the kind of help you're providing your son.

✢

Dear Joseph,

My daughter, who just turned twelve, is quite thin, and her physical development is slow. She has a wonderful personality and is quite popular, but some of the boys are teasing her because she is not as developed as some of the other girls. One of her "friends," a very popular boy, said to me, "You should feed Kelly [obviously not her real name] more fat in her diet. She's so skinny, she makes me sick." I was so shocked that a child would have the audacity to say this to me and, even worse, to say it in front of my daughter. My response to him was "Jason, that's not very nice, and it's very hurtful." My daughter does not want me to speak to his mother, and, so far, I am respecting her wishes. The truth, though, is that I would really like to talk to the boy's mother and let her know what's going on, but ask her not to tell her son that I spoke with her; rather, [I would] ask her to find a way to speak to him without being specific. Any thoughts?

Mother-in-Pain

Dear Mother-in-Pain,

An ancient Jewish teaching compares humiliating a person to murder. For one thing, a humiliated person often wishes that he or she were dead. For another, the damage it inflicts is often irrevocable. For your daughter to hear this boy say, "She's so skinny, she makes me sick," has to be extremely painful, and the hurt of these words may remain with her for years. I know a woman who was told as an adolescent that her backside was so large that it made other people feel like vomiting when they saw her. The woman was in her forties when I heard her speak of this incident, and she said that for years afterward she used to leave a classroom last so that others would not see her from the back. Indeed, the thought that one's physical appearance makes others feel nauseous, as the boy suggested about your daughter, can make one feel nauseous about oneself.

Of course your daughter said she doesn't want you to speak to the boy's mother. When children are ashamed (adults, too), they have a tendency to think that silence will make the issue go away, and that calling attention to it will somehow make it worse. But it won't. You should speak to the mother, because it's unlikely that a boy insensitive enough to say what he said to you, and in your daughter's presence, will be sufficiently shaken by your rather mild rebuke to stop speaking in such a manner. Generally, adults are more aware than children of how devastating these types of humiliation can be, and, unless the mother is totally insensitive, she will be horrified by what her son said, and will make a real effort to ensure that he says nothing like it again.

I therefore believe that you owe it to your daughter to speak to the boy's mother and make her aware of how her son has acted. If you wish, you can ask the mother to try to sensitize her son in a general way, but, from my experience, people who are grossly insensitive do not learn to apply a general critique to a specific situation. I think you will need to run the risk that the mother might make reference to the specific things the boy said.

It's possible that when his mother does speak to him, the boy will realize the cruelty of his words and start acting in a kinder manner. I certainly hope so, for your daughter's sake (though, God willing, as time passes she will become subjected to less of this type of abuse than would be the case if she were very over-weight) and for the sake of all other future victims of this boy's cruel tongue.

Dear Joseph,

You recently highlighted two ethical New Year's resolutions [see pages 259–262], but you said that you had many more. Can you share any that specifically apply to parents and their relations with their children?

Concerned Parent

Dear Concerned Parent,

Here's my New Year's suggestion for parents: Reserve your highest praise of your children for when they perform kind acts. As a general rule, children receive their highest praise for their academic accomplishments (e.g., "My son Sean is so brilliant"), their athletic abilities, their cultural achievements, and, in the case of girls, their looks. Children who receive their greatest compliments in these areas are undoubtedly pleased, but often they also pick up an underlying message: that parental love is somewhat dependent on their continuing to provide their parents with pleasure in these areas. Also, do we really want our children to think that their intelligence, athletic achievement, or appearance is what's really most important about them?

However, the real victim of such a mind-set is the child who isn't that bright, athletic, or good-looking. When does he get his biggest compliment? "Oh, but so-and-so is really a good kid." From which it is apparent that being a good person is not that big a deal.

If children started receiving their highest praise when they performed kind acts, we would raise a generation of people who liked themselves most when they were doing kind things. I can't think of any better, more guaranteed way to improve our world. And your family.

A second suggestion: Make sure you apologize to your children when you hurt their feelings. At workshops I do on character development, I often ask audiences, "How many of you grew up in households where your parents never apologized to you?" Many people raise their hands, and it's clear that even after the passage of many years, the pain of never having received a parental apology still rankles.

Some years ago, when my wife and I were living in Boulder, Colorado, I gave a speech in Denver, and two of my daughters—one then six, the other four—insisted that they wanted to come hear me speak. I thought they were too young, but they were so insistent that I brought them to the speech, proudly introduced them to the audience, and then seated them in the front row.

About ten minutes into the talk, I asked the audience, "How many of you grew up in households where somebody's temper had a bad effect on the house?" To my immense embarrassment and to the audience's great amusement, my six-year-old raised her hand, and then my four-year-old, seeing her older sister's hand go up, raised hers, too. That year I was teaching my six-year-old how to read, and, according to my wife, I am very patient the first time I explain something to somebody, and equally patient the second time. However, by the third time, if I think the person should have understood what I was saying and if he or she hasn't, I can become testy. And that's how I'd been acting toward my daughter. After the speech, I told her two things: "I'm sorry I've snapped at you when you've made mistakes. You weren't doing anything bad, and it was wrong of me to get mad. Please forgive me. Secondly, if I do it in the future, say to me, 'Daddy, you're not supposed to get angry.'" By saying this, I wanted to empower her by giving her something to say when an adult, in this case her father, was unfairly snapping at her.

Parents who never apologize to their children are sending an unfortunate and immoral message: You only have to apologize when you're weak. Parents, of course, make children apologize when they do something wrong, and that's appropriate. But if the parents never say "I'm sorry," then the message being conveyed is that only the weak have to apologize; when you're strong, you don't have to. And certainly no parent wants to teach his or her child such a lesson.

I can assure you that children whose parents apologize when they have acted unfairly will grow up feeling a lot better about themselves and about their parents. So these are my two resolutions: Raise your children to love both themselves and others by reserving your highest praise of your children for when they are kind, and make sure to apologize to your children when you have acted unfairly toward them.

Dear Joseph,

My wife and I, former 1960s flower children, are now suburban parents, soccer mom and dad, the whole nine yards. Our kids are fifteen and twelve. My wife and I smoke pot fairly regularly; twice a week or more. The kids have no clue. We are very careful, and our bedroom is isolated. In front of the kids, we are rabidly antidrug, and I feel guilty about my lack of truthfulness with my children. But, for lots of reasons, we won't give up the weed. What is the ethical path?

Weedies

Dear Weedies,

Are you rabidly antidrug for people aged twelve and fifteen (i.e., for all people under college age), or only for everyone except yourselves? Are you rabidly antidrug for all drugs stronger than marijuana, or for all drugs, including marijuana? My guess would be that you don't think young people should take any drugs whatsoever, and that you probably believe that older people should have the option of smoking pot but should not take any stronger drugs.

If I am correctly assessing your views, then your smoking pot while being antidrug is not ipso facto unethical, although it is of course illegal (and some people may argue that doing something illegal is unethical). It would probably make sense for you to inform your children that while you regard all drug use by minors as unacceptable, you do not feel that way about the use of pot by older people (as long as you truly do restrict your smoking to your bedroom, and certainly never drive after having smoked), because you do not see it as dangerous. And what if they ask you if you use pot? Should you lie? In general, of course, it's better not to lie, but lies cannot always be avoided. For example, if you can't trust your children's discretion, and fear that they might repeat to others that you and your wife smoke pot, you would be wise to keep such information to yourselves. Further, once your children learn that you use pot, it might weaken their resistance to doing so, even at their relatively young ages. In addition, even though I'm no fan of lying, it would generally be unwise for a father or mother who commits adultery to make that fact known to his or her children. Which means that the parent would probably have to lie to his or her children if questioned about it directly. (Of course, one could make the case that you should not engage in behavior that you will feel compelled to lie about.) Similarly, a man who preaches to his children to be honest in their dealings with others probably will, and perhaps should, lie if his children ask him if he lives by the standards he demands from them, and he doesn't. In lying, however, you run the risk that if your children learn one day that the two of you are pretty regular pot smokers, they may regard you as liars and hypocrites, and feel a diminished respect for you.

So what should you do? It would probably be best to stop smoking pot. If that's not going to happen, then you should probably continue acting as you are, although you should find ways to make it known to your children that you do not regard pot-smoking by adults with the same abhorrence you regard all other drug use. Your saying this will at least help protect you from the charge of hypocrisy when your children find out (and they probably will) that you are pot smokers.

THREE

Friends

Dear Joseph,

My best girlfriend of twenty years married a man who had a major crush on me for about seven years. I am very happily married and have three beautiful children. My husband's work commitments are taking him out of town for the next four weeks. My friend's husband has made it more than clear that he wants to take my husband's place while he is gone—with me, that is. I have never been interested in him, much less now that I am happily married. I told him all this, but he still persists in making rude comments. My girlfriend is the only person I have to call on right now to help me with the children. I don't want to jeopardize our friendship, but should I tell her the truth, or should I continue to ignore it?

Pestered

Dear Pestered,

I'm going to do something I've never done in one of these columns—offer two responses to your question. I wrote the first a day or two after I received your letter, at a time when the answer to what you should do seemed obvious:

If there is no chance that you are misreading the man's intentions, and if you have told the man to desist from trying to convince you to commit adultery, and he has refused to, then it seems to me that you should say something to your girlfriend. Admittedly, this is a tricky situation, and she might well disbelieve you and end your friendship (it might even become more unpleasant; the man might claim that it was you who was "coming on" to him, which would be reminiscent of the untruthful wife of Potiphar in Genesis, who asserted that it was Joseph who tried to rape her rather than she who tried to seduce him). But the fact is that although this man knows you are married and are a good friend of his wife, he still tries to entice you into a sexual relationship, and this reveals a deep character flaw, one that his spouse is entitled to be aware of. The Golden Rule seems to apply here: Wouldn't you want to know if your husband was trying to convince your closest friend to become involved with him?

Generally, I'm not a believer in getting involved in the intimate details of other people's lives. But I believe that when dealing with so flagrant a violation of personal decency, such behavior should be revealed to the one person who should know about it.

Still, one thing in the tone of your letter disturbed me: the implication that because your friend is the only one who can help you with your children, you don't want to do anything that might jeopardize your friendship. Your decision about whether to tell your friend about her husband's behavior should not be based on your needing her help with your children, but on your conclusion that this is the right thing to do. Thus, it would be cynical, rather than an act of friendship, if you waited until you no longer needed her help to tell her about her husband.

A few days after I wrote this, I was in Miami to give a speech. The talk was preceded by a dinner at which I was seated with four couples. I told them about this letter and shared my response with them. I was shaken by their almost uniform rejection of the advice I had offered, particularly from the women present. Several of them questioned whether you had discouraged the man's advances firmly enough, and wondered why you were still spending time alone with him (obviously he was not making these suggestive comments to you in the presence of others). With one exception, the people with whom I spoke deemed it unwise to tell your friend; the couple had probably worked out how to conduct their marriage, and any comments you made to the wife would likely have only one result—the end of your friendship.

Under my prodding, almost all of them agreed that if the man were not married to your friend but that they were dating, or even engaged, then it would be appropriate for you to speak up. Revealing information that would save someone from marrying a person of such low character was considered as wise and just. Sharing information that could lead to the breakup of an already existent marriage was not.

My final advice is something of an amalgamation of all that I heard: Make sure you're very firm with the man about not crossing boundaries, and avoid being alone with him at all times. Tell your husband about your situation, and tell this man that you have done so. With the clear understanding that his behavior was now coming under greater scrutiny (I think he would understand that if he didn't shape up, the next person to be told after your husband would be his wife), I think he might finally cease and desist.

Dear Joseph,

I just wrote a letter, but I'm having second thoughts about sending it. It's to a friend of mine, a person who somehow seems to bring out the worst in me. When I'm with him, I become sarcastic, and often a little nasty. So I wrote him that it would be better if we weren't friends any longer. Now I find I'm feeling guilty at the thought of sending the letter and ending our friendship. What do you think?

Confused

Dear Confused,

Years ago, I found myself growing increasingly frustrated and annoyed with an old friend. It seemed that whenever we were together, our conversation quickly degenerated into banter and humorous insults. I found that I no longer looked forward to seeing him; it was tiresome and annoying to spend time in his company. One day, I said to him, "I don't know why this has happened, but it seems that whenever I'm with you, you turn every comment I make into a joke and throw insults at me."

My friend was taken aback. "I'll tell you the truth," he said. "I've been feeling for a while that that's what you've been doing, and I've been getting pretty sick of it, too."

I'm very grateful that we had that conversation. To this day, I don't know how this silly and annoying quality had been introduced into our relationship (I still suspect he was more responsible for it than I, and he undoubtedly feels the reverse), but once we spoke about it, the nature of our social communication immediately changed for the better.

So before mailing your letter, I would speak to the person involved. If you find it difficult to *say* these things to your friend, then maybe express the thought through a letter or e-mail, but one written in a very different tone. Tell him what is making you unhappy, and what you'd like to see change.

If your friendship has been a good one, then I suspect such a conversation or letter will make this person sad, so that he'll try to undo the damage that has been done to your friendship. But what if your attempt to heal the breach is unsuccessful—if your friend thinks you're oversensitive and overreacting, and has no desire to change his behavior? In such a case, my instinct would be to terminate the relationship at least temporarily. There are people who really don't bring out the best in us. For example, some individuals are very cutting in their comments about others so that we find ourselves becoming more critical of other people when we are with them. In fact, we become concerned that if we speak sweetly of others in their presence, we will sound naive. The same applies to cynics and others who mock and mistrust other people's ideals and righteous actions. Such people have a pernicious effect because they make goodness itself seem pointless. And, in your case, you find that in the presence of this person you become sarcastic and often angry. As I have long concluded, life is too short to spend with people who neither bring us pleasure nor help us grow and become better human beings.

Of course, sometimes the person who has a negative impact on us is one to whom we are intimately related, such as a parent or sibling, and with whom we can't cut off contact. In such a case, try to convey your concerns to the person so that you can raise the relationship to a higher level. But if you can't bring about such a change, then limit—but don't eliminate—contact, so as to preserve your sanity. Such advice applies particularly to a close relative who is overly critical.

However, in an instance in which the negative relationship is with someone you don't need to be in contact with, then, if you don't succeed in improving the relationship, try to eliminate, to the extent possible, that person's presence in your life. One should seek out for friends people who inspire you to be a better person, and in whose presence you feel better about yourself, not worse. Anything less is masochistic and self-destructive.

Dear Joseph,

I sometimes get together with a group of guys whom I grew up with. One of the men always had a tendency to exaggerate, but now he tells outright lies. For example, if he introduces me to someone, he might say, "My mother and his mother go way back—they went to kindergarten together," when that's simply not true. Or if someone says he slept badly, he might say, "I've been up for three nights straight." This wild exaggerating/lying seems like a bad habit he's gotten into in order to impress people or to supposedly make the conversation more interesting. But I feel he should be committed to telling the truth. Do you think I should just avoid being with him, let it slide, or confront him?

Righteous or Self-Righteous?

Dear Righteous or Self-Righteous?

Let me start at the end, with your letter's concluding sentence. You suggest three possible responses toward your increasingly hyperbolic and lying friend:

avoidance, letting the matter slide, and confrontation. I want to analyze the benefits and disadvantages of each so that you'll understand how I arrived at what I think is the most ethically appropriate response.

1. *Avoid being with him.* Sometimes, when someone has done something that hurts or annoys us, if we avoid the person for a short period, we can resume the relationship with little, if any, residue of ill will. In such cases, temporary avoidance seems a wise response. However, in this instance, your friend's propensity to exaggerate and lie is well established and seems to be growing worse. So any time you resume the relationship this annoying trait will resurface and further alienate you. Therefore, "avoiding" your friend will simply turn into a euphemism for ending the relationship, one that has endured for many years and presumably has brought you much pleasure. To end so long-standing a relationship without making at least one effort to fix it seems unfair both to you and to your friend.

2. *Let it slide.* In theory this sounds possible, but in practice it won't work. I do believe in letting certain annoying traits slide; otherwise no friendships, or marriages for that matter, would last. But when possible, I try to find a way to mitigate the annoyance. For example, I become very irritated at people who habitually arrive late for meetings, particularly when I'm waiting for them on a street corner. So now, when I schedule a meeting with someone who habitually

runs late, I arrange to meet the person at a bookstore. That way, while waiting for him or her, I'm looking at books instead of at my watch. In effect, that's one way to let the matter slide.

But here, it's clear that your friend's silly untruths are a sufficiently bothersome trait, and one that cannot easily be ignored. If you try to let the matter slide, you'll only find yourself gritting your teeth a lot, until one day you explode and say things that probably will inflict great pain and end the relationship.

3. *Confront him.* An unpleasant strategy to be sure, but the only one of the three responses that has more upside than downside potential. You strike me as a good candidate for offering criticism, since I have the impression that you somewhat dread the prospect of doing so. That makes it more likely that your friend will see that you are reluctant to offer criticism, and will recognize the goodwill behind your words.

If you choose the third option, tell your friend —obviously in private—that hearing him make a statement like "My mother and his mother went to kindergarten together" makes you uncomfortable. Add that comments like this make it hard for you to enjoy being with him because you can't tell when he is giving you information you can rely on and when he is speaking merely for effect, and so should be ignored. Ask him if he's willing to try to make a real effort for three days to speak accurately (I wouldn't use the word *truthfully* because that will make him defensive). Also, ask him whether it would be all right with him if the next time you hear him telling tall tales you could signal him, let's say, by raising your hand to form a stop sign.

Make two things clear to your friend: You really like him (this will give him a positive motivation to change, so as to gain your approval—apparently, trying to gain others' approval is behind a lot of his untruths) and that it's really important for his credibility that he make this change. Either he'll ignore your advice and your friendship likely will end, or he will change (maybe not as much as you would like, but enough to enable you to enjoy his company again), and one day he'll really thank you.

Good luck!

Postscript: A reader recalled how a confrontation in a similar situation didn't go well at the time it occurred, but ultimately turned out to be worthwhile: "I have a very dear friend who . . . exaggerates and stretches the truth to the point where she has done everything, and knows everything about everything. She also is very stubborn. I and another pal confronted her about six years ago, and she was very defensive, but I'll tell you, the exaggerations have decreased phenomenally."

Dear Joseph,

I hurt a friend so profoundly that I know there is no chance of friendship again. I want to apologize, but I don't know how. I don't expect forgiveness, but still would like to try. Help!

A Lost Soul

Dear Lost Soul,

My heart goes out to you. Whatever you did, I can't help but be moved by the depth of guilt and pain you're experiencing. If indeed the hurt you inflicted is as profound as you say, then it is possible that all you can do now is send your friend a copy of the letter you sent me. That way, he or she will at least be aware of how sorry you feel for what you did. If you don't get a response, don't push the matter, at least not for quite a while. Your friend might need time to recuperate from the hurt you inflicted.

In the Jewish religion, there is a tradition to approach people whom one has hurt before the beginning of the Jewish New Year (generally in September), and to express regret and ask for forgiveness. Having such a specified period each year to seek reconciliation makes it easier for the offender, who, like you, is generally embarrassed by what he or she has done, to approach the person who's been hurt.

Maybe it would be a good idea for the United States to institute a National Apology Day, during which people could try to reconnect with those whom they've hurt, and beg forgiveness. Perhaps such a day could be scheduled in December, thereby enabling people to finish the year reconciled with each other, and to start the new year with something approaching a clean slate.

One final thought: Why don't you write in a journal what you have done (write it now, while you still feel ashamed about it and can write without rationalizing) and what you have learned about yourself from this incident. Obviously, the goal of such self-analysis is to ensure that you never act in a similar way again.

Dear Joseph,

I was hired by a yoga center to establish a comprehensive program for them. At the instruction of my boss, I hired several top-notch yoga teachers. The center struggled for a few months, but never got off the ground. A few weeks ago, my boss left—he told me he was fired by the center's owners—and now the various yoga teachers, many of whom are my friends, haven't been paid for their last weeks of work. The total money owed them is almost $4,000. I called my ex-boss, who told me he's in no position to pay, nor does he have the legal responsibility to do so. Meanwhile, the people who bought the center have already closed down the yoga program and argue that they bear no financial responsibility for debts incurred by the previous owners. I know I don't have a legal obligation to pay these people, but since they took this job because I recruited them, do I have a moral responsibility to pay the money they are owed? If I did, it would wipe out almost all my savings, but if I don't, I don't know how I am going to look them in the eye.

Feeling Guilty

Dear Feeling Guilty,

Obviously, your friends have a legitimate legal case against the center's owners and possibly against your ex-boss, who hired them. But since each of them is probably owed only several hundred dollars (based on your calculation that the total is less than $4,000), I doubt it is worthwhile for them to hire a lawyer to pursue the case (the amounts of money involved are probably too low for a lawyer to deem it worthwhile to take such a case on a contingency basis). Within a matter of an hour, maybe two, the legal fees would probably be more than any sum he might recover. On the other hand, perhaps there is a service in your community offering low-priced legal services for people of modest means.

Regarding *your* responsibility, I would argue that it should be determined by your intentions. If your intentions were pure—that is, you assumed that the boss for whom you were working was honest and that he would pay them—I don't think anyone can hold you responsible. Only if you had substantial reason to assume that this man might be crooked or unreliable should you have refrained from working for him, and from recruiting others. As a matter of tact, however, I would call up each of the teachers, explain the circumstances, and apologize for having

141

gotten them into this difficult situation. But I do not believe you are morally culpable, and I would not suggest that you bring hardship upon yourself by wiping out all your savings to pay off a debt incurred by your boss.

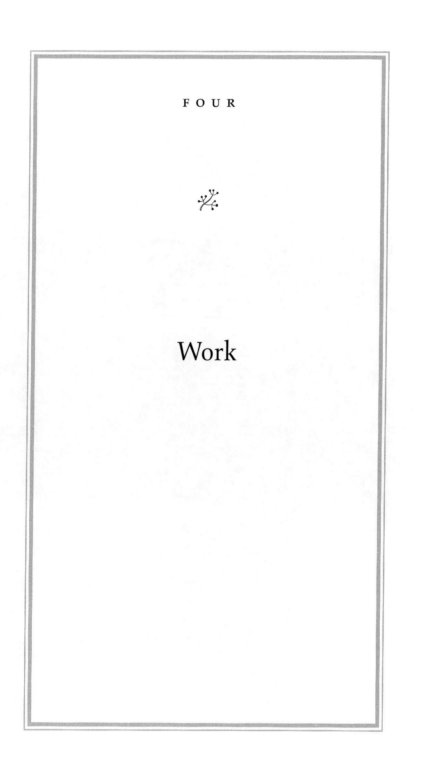

FOUR

Work

Dear Joseph,

I teach high-school math in Maine. Last year, our state enacted a law requiring fingerprinting of all teachers as a condition of certification. I was quite outspoken against the law, believing that for teachers currently employed it goes against the idea that one is innocent until proven guilty. Also, the law seems to violate the constitutional prohibition against unreasonable search and seizure. When I shared my feelings with my students, they were worried that when I came up for recertification, I would become one of the "refusers"—teachers who refuse to get fingerprinted and hence can't be recertified. Well, I submitted to the fingerprinting last week, and now feel like a hypocrite. I gave in because I love teaching and my current job, and moving from the state is out of the question. I am still quite upset by the law, and am having a hard time resolving whether my opposition to it is made less legitimate by complying with it. Can you help me?

An Almost Refuser

Dear Almost Refuser,

Continue to oppose the law, and don't feel that you're a hypocrite. A sense of proportion dictates that one doesn't have to make tremendous personal sacrifices on behalf of every position one takes. After all, you're not being asked to support a Nazi, Communist, or racist regime. Rather, you believe it's wrong for the state to require the fingerprinting of teachers.

I happen to disagree with your reasoning that such a procedure goes against the idea of "innocent until proven guilty." If such were the case, then it would mean, for example, that any time a murder is committed and police ask all people who have been in the house where the crime occurred to submit to fingerprinting, a presumption is being made that they are guilty. Rather, what the police and government are seeking is a technique that will help them capture guilty people and exonerate innocent ones.

Having said that, I do understand, if not necessarily agree with, those who find this law overly intrusive. But I don't see it as being of such moral seriousness as to require one to destroy one's professional career. Unless you are intending to commit a serious crime while not wearing gloves, I would continue to teach and continue to express your opposition to this law.

$\frac{y}{f}$

Dear Joseph,

My conscience bothers me because a small portion of my work concerns supporting and advertising weapons research. Is it ethical to support such research?

Concerned Weapons Worker

Dear Concerned Weapons Worker,

Weapons research is not, in and of itself, immoral. Indeed, if moral people assumed that it were, then the armies of the most evil regimes in history would have triumphed in every war they fought. World War II would have ended in a Nazi takeover of the world, and the Cold War would have ended with a world ruled by totalitarian Communist governments. For that matter, if you take your argument to its logical conclusion, then American society would be destroyed by criminals in possession of far more sophisticated weapons than the police have.

So the larger question for you to address is, Are the people for whom I am engaging in this research doing it on behalf of evil governments that will use these weapons to murder, terrorize, or subjugate innocent people? If they are, then any help you provide, even if it is only a small portion of your work, is unethical. But if the work is being performed on behalf of democratic regimes, and the weapons will be directed against those who use armaments against the innocent or to undermine lawful regimes, then such work is not immoral.

✻

Dear Joseph,

I have severe repetitive-strain injury, which means that I need some fairly expensive equipment to work comfortably at any office job. Is it okay not to mention my condition at a job interview to avoid risking discrimination? A friend with cancer tells me that the people she met at a prominent cancer hospital advised her never to tell prospective employers that she has cancer. But if I hide my condition, I might make my bosses angry in my first week when they find out how much my condition will cost them.

Painfully Ambivalent

Dear Painfully Ambivalent,

In the well-known words of Søren Kierkegaard, the nineteenth-century Danish philosopher, I answer your question with "fear and trembling," and uncertainty. My gut instinct is that you shouldn't go out of your way to mention your disability in advance, and then, when you show up for work, you should offer— if this is at all a feasible possibility—to pay, or split, the cost of the additional equipment that is required.

It seems to me that if the would-be employer is not permitted by law to ask questions concerning your condition, you're not obligated to offer such information. Why then the fear and trembling and uncertainty on my part? Because withholding information that will cost your employer money is somewhat deceitful (at least by omission). It is also quite likely that you will be regarded in the future as a slightly untrustworthy person.

Others whom I've consulted inform me that the larger the company to which you are applying for a position, the greater the reason to be open about your condition. Large companies are more likely to hire people with disabilities. Conversely, the smaller the company, the more your offer to assume some of the costs of the needed equipment will make a positive impression.

In discussing your letter with many people, I received a large variety of responses, many articulated with great, and contradictory, vehemence. One woman, who had long helped promote legislation to protect those with disabilities, insisted that such legislation was intended to free such people from having to be secretive about their condition. On the other hand, a friend in the human-resources department at a national company insisted that it would be very disadvantageous to offer information about a nonapparent disability up front.

I hope what I have said helps you, but the truth is, I'm not 100 percent comfortable with all that I've written, and I'm ready and willing to consider alternative positions.

Postscript: Unfortunately, no one wrote in to suggest any possibilities not discussed in my response. So, I suppose, my fear and trembling and imperfect suggestion are currently doomed to remain as they were.

✼

Dear Joseph,

As a high-school teacher, I am often asked to write letters of recommendation for students. When the students are people I really don't have a high regard for, I usually can find a way to get out of it. But then there are the students who are pretty competent, but not extraordinarily so. My problem is that I know many other people write highly exaggerated letters of recommendation, so that if I give a frank assessment of the people on whose behalf I'm writing, my letter might well do them more harm than good. I don't want to lie, and I don't want to hurt their chances of admission. What should I do?

Confused

Dear Confused,

A Jewish joke tells of a synagogue president checking into the references of a cantor who's applied for a position at the synagogue. He calls up the president of the previous congregation at which the cantor worked, and the man tells him, "This cantor is like Abraham, like Moses, like an angel!" They hang up, and on the spot the president calls the cantor and hires him.

At the Sabbath service a few days later, when the cantor sings, his voice is awful. He warbles, and can barely carry a tune. In addition, he displays a bad temper.

Sunday morning, the outraged president calls up the man who gave him the recommendation. "What do you mean comparing this man to Abraham, Moses, and an angel? He was awful, and not a nice person to boot."

"But everything I said is true," the other man insists. "Abraham couldn't sing, and this cantor can't sing. Moses was a stutterer [the common understanding of Exodus 4:10], and this cantor is a stutterer. An angel is not a mensch [Yiddish for both "human being" and "a decent person"], and this cantor is not a mensch."

This joke identifies a problem routinely encountered by those who rely on letters of recommendation: How do they decide whether or not the letters are accurate? My guess is that most letters of recommendation are taken with a grain of salt, since those receiving the letters know that they are often filled with hyperbole.

So should you write words you believe to be true but which might damage the applicant's chances, or write something that you feel is untruthful? I would do the following: Write in a manner that you feel is true, focusing on the applicant's greatest strengths, but add a few lines such as "I want you to know that I support so-and-so's application, and have engaged in no exaggeration. I have added this sentence because I know that many people do make exaggerated statements in such letters. The good things, though, that I have written about so-and-so can be fully relied upon."

I suspect that a letter like this will make a good and helpful impression. Which is exactly what you wish to do—help the applicant, while not violating your own principles.

Dear Joseph,

I am a hairdresser in New York City and cater to both female and male clients. It often happens that customers either cancel at the last minute (when it's too late to replace them), or just don't show up. Then, a few days later, they schedule another appointment, and either make passing reference, or no reference at all, to the appointment they missed. I can count on the fingers of one hand the number of customers who have offered to pay for the missed appointment. Yet to me the loss is serious, because when someone doesn't show up, I lose income that I need, and could have had (there are many times when I have turned down other customers because of this booking). Do I have the right to charge people who cancel at the last moment or are no-shows?

Frustrated and Furious

Dear Frustrated and Furious,

It has long been known that most analysts and therapists have a policy of charging patients for missed appointments (unless the patients give at least twenty-four hours notice). I've heard therapists explain that such a policy is necessary to teach those who come to them to be responsible. I suspect that their real and justifiable reason for charging "no-shows" is that these therapists feel that they are entitled to the money that they expected to earn, and which they would otherwise lose through no fault of their own. After all, if the patient does not come for the appointment, it is her fault. Why then should the therapist bear the financial loss?

Of course you have a right to ask people to compensate you for the money that you expected to earn, and for the time you set aside to work on their hair. I would suggest that you institute the following policy. From now on, when you or your receptionist books an appointment, make the following statement: "If you are going to have to cancel an appointment, please contact our office at least twenty-four hours in advance. Otherwise, because it will be too late for us to book another appointment, we will be forced to charge you for the time we set aside for you."

What will happen? I suspect that some people who do miss an appointment will not call to reschedule so as to avoid having to make this payment, and you will lose them as customers. As regards those who do reschedule, when they come in, I would suggest that as a matter of tact and goodwill, you not charge them the first time they miss an appointment; just remind them of your policy, and insist on payment only the second time it happens (my dentist did this to me when I missed an appointment—I suppose the thought of having a tooth drilled is what caused me to forget—and I felt very grateful to him for his good-natured and understanding attitude).

That only a handful of people have ever offered to pay you is a sad reflection of the extent to which so many people are insensitive to the needs of others. When people book an appointment with you, they have a right to expect that you'll be there for them. Why, then, should you not have the right to expect the same from them?

Dear Joseph,

An evangelical Christian author who was having a severe writing block needed someone to help develop a novel that has a potentially huge audience. Looking at his outline, I feared some elements of the book might be offensive, so I said I could not do the job, although I was broke. The agent begged me to take it, insisting that if I were involved, I could keep those elements out of the text. After meeting with the author and making my own views crystal clear, I determined that I could indeed control the content. But while I could have kept this particular book from spreading an offensive message, I feared that I might be helping to advance a brand of Christianity that I know to be explicitly anti-Catholic. I am a Catholic. Should I have taken this writing gig?

Still Broke

Dear Still Broke,

Some years ago, I wrote a series of three murder mysteries. While researching one, I got involved in a discussion with a pharmacist, who mentioned to me some poisons that were very difficult to identify; in other words, if someone were murdered by one of these poisons, the police would be unlikely to identify the death as a homicide. For plot reasons, I was very tempted to have the murderer in my novel use this poison, but I decided not to do so. I feared that if I described the poison some reader might use this information to commit a murder.

Was I being overly fastidious? Perhaps, but the thought that I could in any way help cause damage to an innocent person was a major deterrent to me. Therefore, I understand why you would not want to use your literary talents to help write a novel whose author might then use his increased popularity to spread a message that you feel is anti-Catholic. Leni Riefenstahl might insist that she was not a Nazi. But her use of her considerable artistic talents on behalf of the Nazis (in 1935 she produced *Triumph of the Will*, a compelling film record of a Nazi rally in Nuremberg that vividly illustrated Hitler's charismatic appeal) helped increase the popularity of Hitler and the Nazi party in Germany and throughout the world. Deservedly, she has been held in widespread contempt ever since.

So my question to you is: How certain are you that the writer for whom you would have worked, and the people with whom he associates, are anti-Catholic?

Do they see the Pope, as classical Catholic-haters have, as a devilish figure in alliance with Satan or as involved in a Catholic conspiracy to dominate the United States and/or the world? Do they advocate any abridgement of Catholic rights in the United States? Do they actively discourage their followers from voting for Catholics, even Catholic candidates who might share some views with them, because of their anti-Catholic bias? If they are bigots of that sort, then, by refusing to work for such people, you unquestionably have acted in a morally appropriate manner.

If this writer's anti-Catholicism is far more muted than that, then you probably could have worked for him without compromising your moral integrity. Perhaps you could even have influenced him to become a bit more moderate in his views. Still, I believe that you did the right thing—which is particularly commendable because you so needed the money—in not wanting to help advance a cause that you feel will spread intolerant brands of religiosity.

Dear Joseph,

A friend of mine asked me recently whether she should accept a job with the FBI because that might be interpreted as supporting our government. She is bitterly opposed to this administration and its policies, but badly needs an income. What would you advise?

Puzzled

Dear Puzzled,

During the time Rudolph Giuliani was New York City's mayor, it was no secret that he was not widely popular in the African-American community. Yet I don't recall hearing that black police officers felt morally constrained to leave the police force, or that other blacks felt similarly constrained not to join it. One could dislike Giuliani (I thought he was a very good mayor) and still work in the police department without suffering from an ongoing crisis of conscience.

Similarly, Bill Clinton was not the most beloved president in military circles. Again, this did not lead to the widespread resignation of army officers or to a lack of recruits.

Your friend, you tell me, is bitterly opposed to the current president and his administration. So what? Among the primary responsibilities of those employed by the FBI is the apprehension of dangerous criminals and the stopping of would-be terrorists from carrying out attacks inside the United States. If your friend finds that these tasks appeal to her, she should feel free to work for the FBI. As long as our country remains a democracy, and doesn't become authoritarian or totalitarian or use the FBI to try and destroy people because of their political views, an individual should feel free to work for the FBI. However, if your friend's dislike of the administration is so great that she believes that the president is trying to take America in an authoritarian or totalitarian direction, then I would urge her not to join the FBI; I would regard such a mind-set as paranoiac and I would not trust the judgment of a law-enforcement official who held such views.

Therefore, as long as your friend sees her responsibility in working for the FBI as fighting against those who threaten "domestic tranquility," she should be able to do a good and moral job, no matter which president is in office. On the other hand, her views about the administration would make her a poor candidate to work for the CIA, but I have a feeling she already knows that.

FIVE

Money

Dear Joseph,

Living in New York City, I am daily confronted —sometimes it feels like hounded—with requests from beggars. When I just pass beggars by, I feel uncomfortable with myself. Yet, should I give them money, knowing as we all do that many of them will probably use the money to buy drugs or liquor?

Guilty in the Big Apple

Dear Guilty in the Big Apple,

I know few people who have a consistent policy regarding donations to beggars. Those who believe one should readily give to beggars rarely wind up handing out coins to everyone who asks them. In many parts of New York City, where I, too, live, such a policy would cause one to be giving to people about every two minutes, a very time-consuming and expensive

161

proposition. Years ago, when begging was still common in the city's subways, my wife and I once were confronted by so many beggars that I commented, "It would have been cheaper had we gone by taxi."

On the other hand, I find it hard, if not impossible, to walk past a person who says to me, "I'm hungry. Could you give me money so I could get something to eat?" My mother, Helen Telushkin, gives money to all beggars who tell her that they are hungry. She has told me that when she feels hungry, she finds the pangs so painful that she can't imagine not helping a person who's craving food.

But what if the person soliciting the money is lying, if he or she just wants your money to buy alcohol or drugs? In such a case, if I give the money, I will have been fooled.

The question, therefore, is, what is preferable— to avoid giving to anyone, including those who truly are hungry, because some beggars are deceivers, or to give to all who claim hunger, knowing that some are liars? To me, the latter course seems preferable. As the Christian theologian and writer C. S. Lewis wrote, "It will not bother me in the hour of death to reflect that I have been 'had for a sucker' by any number of impostors; but it would be a torment to know that one had refused even one person in need."

Postscript: The potential misuse of donations by beggars troubled most, but not all, of my correspondents. One wrote, "If I give money, who am I to dictate how it is spent? I personally enjoy the odd beer or two, and would be deeply offended if someone requested that I not spend money at the pub." Another reader also felt that one has no moral responsibility to monitor how the money is spent: "If you give from the heart, your reward will be in heaven. If beggars accept your gift under false pretenses, it is between them and heaven."

But several other respondents, probably fearing that their money would be used for something stronger and more self-destructive than the "odd beer or two," have devised stratagems to avoid such misuse: "I wouldn't give money to beggars lest they use it to purchase alcohol or drugs. However, a charitable gesture would be to buy them a sandwich and non-alcoholic beverage."

One reader had a highly practical suggestion: "I wish this city had a program . . . where some restaurants would sell vouchers for meals, which you could carry around and give to beggars." It seems to me that this idea is a highly moral one, but perhaps workable only for take-out orders; most restaurants wouldn't want to have beggars, who often are not clean or properly dressed, sitting down at their tables. Is such an attitude itself elitist and immoral? I don't think so. Restaurants are in business to make money, and if having beggars come in regularly alienates many customers, they have the right to discourage such "traffic," although they should give the beggars food-to-go.

I know that some readers might argue that my response is itself elitist and note that, fifty years ago, restaurants in the South justified their refusal to serve African-American patrons with a similar argument, that if black people came into a restaurant, white people would stay away. But the cases are not analogous. Not permitting people to sit down in a restaurant because of their skin color or religion is immoral and should never be justified, even to make money. Discriminating against people because of their behavior (such as not practicing personal hygiene or not wearing appropriate clothing) is not.

Dear Joseph,

Last October, I got a call from an elderly woman whose house I'd cleaned briefly. The movers were coming in the morning, she told me, and she asked me to sleep over and I did. Now she calls me three times a day and stays on the phone for more than an hour. Besides her need for friendship, she needs someone to take her shopping, etc., and I have helped with that. She gives me $7 for gas. I told her last night that I get paid for doing what I do for her. In addition to the phone calls, she now calls me "daughter." I don't know her at all except for when I met her to clean her house. I can't leave her because she has no one, I mean no one. I am asking for more than $7. Please help direct me spiritually.

Very Frazzled

Dear Very Frazzled,

You have a right to be upset. This woman's situation is indeed pitiable, but her unwillingness to recognize appropriate boundaries seems to be making your life somewhat pitiable as well. Calling a person you barely know three times a day, and repeatedly asking for favors, is inappropriate (she might, of course, be mentally disturbed).

You write that the woman is alone. Does this mean that she truly has no family, or are they perhaps alienated from her? If she does have close relatives, I would find out their names and call them. Also, find out if there are groups in your city that extend help to those who are homebound or who need assistance with driving and shopping, and put her in touch with them.

Finally, though, I have a question for you. If this woman paid you a fair wage, would you then be willing to maintain this relationship? If so, figure out what compensation would cause you to continue the relationship, and request it. While I understand your feelings of guilt about abandoning her, her behavior at this point has become, albeit unintentionally, far too demanding, and perhaps even abusive. And you have the moral and spiritual right to protect yourself from such behavior.

Dear Joseph,

A few months back, I read an article by Peter Singer, the world-renowned Princeton philosophy professor, arguing that the major ethical demand of our time is to feed the hungry and provide for the basic needs of the world's poor. He maintained that since the average American family can get by on $30,000 a year, each family has a moral obligation to give any earnings above that amount to charities that help relieve world hunger.

So a family earning $50,000 a year should give $20,000 to, say, Oxfam America. If they earn $100,000, they should donate $70,000. In Singer's view, to spend $100 on a restaurant meal for two when others are starving is not only immoral but tantamount to standing by while someone is dying and doing nothing to help. As resistant as I am to Singer's thinking—I certainly don't want to give away so much of my income to charity—his logic seems compelling, doesn't it?

Guilty and Well-Fed

Dear Guilty and Well-Fed,

Having also read Peter Singer's argument that people are morally obligated to donate a substantial part, and perhaps most, of their earnings to the hungry and poor ("The Singer Solution to World Poverty," *The New York Times Magazine*), I'm not persuaded.

First, it seems to me that an ethical argument detailing human obligations must also take into account human nature. And this is precisely what Singer is ignoring. In effect, he's asking people, once their earnings exceed a certain level, to work full-time on behalf of strangers. But other than to practice the most extraordinary and unusual altruism, what would motivate a person to earn more than $30,000, since anything over that would, in effect, be "taxed" at 100 percent?

Since many people would rather relax than work, it seems to me that Singer's proposal would discourage human initiative. Wouldn't it be more moral to take human nature into account and simply encourage people, particularly as they become more affluent, to give more of their income to charity, rather than to make a demand that almost all people will ignore as being ridiculous?

Second, once one accepts Singer's premise that people are morally obligated to donate all excess income to the needy, there's almost no end to the demands one can make of them. For example, Singer chooses to earn his living as a philosopher at Princeton. I have no idea what he's earning there, but let's guess it's $100,000 a year. Let's also say that if Professor Singer were to become a commodities broker, he could earn $300,000 a year. By his reasoning, it seems to me that he would be morally obligated to take whatever job paid the most so that he would be in a position to help more of those people who might otherwise starve. After all, what moral right should one have to practice the profession one wants if, by practicing another, more people's lives could be saved?

Another objection to Singer's reasoning is suggested by Dennis Prager. If Singer's thinking were to become widespread, the upshot would be a significant rise in unemployment. Clearly, a world in which people choose to live without frills so that they can donate their excess income to charity would be one in which, for example, no one would eat out except at "greasy spoons," no one would go to the opera or to theaters, since tickets are so costly, and no one would buy expensive fountain pens. Certainly, no one would attend elite schools like Princeton, where tuition and expenses alone amount to well over $30,000 a year. It so happens that many, many people work in jobs creating items that are not essential for survival. In Singer's scenario, all such businesses would close down, the workers would be discharged (and might soon find themselves in need of charity), and all luxury items would eventually disappear from the face of the earth.

What would be the upshot of Singer's plan to cure world hunger? A world in which most people, deprived of material rewards for working harder, would work less (and therefore have less income to give away), a world in which people would be morally obligated to make career decisions based on pay and not on personal desire, and a world in which all goods beyond life's basic necessities would be viewed as decadent and immoral.

World poverty and hunger are serious problems and require serious, but also *feasible,* solutions. Obviously, in addition to encouraging efforts among the poor that could help remedy or mitigate their poverty (for example, making birth-control information and devices readily available so that poor families don't have more children than they can afford to raise, and providing job training that prepares people to earn decent wages), we should try to motivate people who have more than enough to give away more, but not all, of their excess income to charities that help the poor.

A wise principle in Jewish law states that "a decree may not be imposed on the community unless the majority can bear it." Thus, according to Jewish law, one is expected to give at least 10 percent of his net income to charity, but not more than 20 percent, lest the giver become poor. Obviously, there are people who can afford to give more than 20 percent, but they are the uncommon exceptions.

It strikes me as both more moral and helpful to the hungry and poor to make reasonable demands of people (such as those that insist on far higher levels of giving than is the prevailing norm) than it is to make utopian demands that will be ignored.

Still, I think we should thank Professor Singer for prompting people to think about whether to donate more to charities that help the truly needy. I have long been moved by the words of C. S. Lewis, who wrote in *Mere Christianity*, "If our charities do not at all pinch or hamper us, I should say they are too small. There ought to be things we should like to do and cannot do because our charitable expenditures exclude them."

Dear Joseph,

A recent *New York Times* article described a man who bought a $7,000 hot tub, then spent an additional $11,000 to hire a company to haul the hot tub up to his apartment, on the forty-third floor, I think. Obviously, everything the man did was legal, but is it moral, in a world filled with poverty, to waste money on oneself like that?

Outraged

Dear Outraged,

Judaism, the religion I know best, expects a person [as I have noted] to give 10 percent of his after-tax income to charity. I think it is a good idea for a religion to designate a set percentage rather than simply issue a general admonition to its practitioners to be charitable. For one thing, most people will give more money if a percentage is specified. In the absence of such a requirement, many people will consider themselves to be charitable, although they give less, often much less. Second, I think that designating 10 percent sends an implicit message that once you have given that amount, you need not feel guilty about how you spend the rest. When I saw the article in the *Times,* I admit that I, too, felt that so large an expenditure on a hot tub was excessive. But for me, the more pertinent question is: Does this man give a significant percentage of his income to charity? If he does, then he should have the moral right to spend his money as he pleases. If he doesn't, then he is acting selfishly, whether he spends his money hauling a hot tub up forty-three flights or deposits the money in a savings account.

Postscript: David Szonyi, a friend and longtime worker in philanthropic organizations, found my reasoning flawed: "Shouldn't there be an ethics of consumption as well as an ethics of charity? Is there such a thing as excessive conspic-uous consumption? What if a man or woman commis-sioned a gold-plated hot tub for $50,000 or $100,000? Are we obligated not to flaunt our wealth? Also, and perhaps more important, the more a person lavishes material goods on himself, the less he or she probably has available to give to charity, or to help create new wealth that will generate more funds for charity."

After mulling over Mr. Szonyi's response, I find my-self in the position of the rabbi confronted by two litigants. After hearing out the first party, he said to the man, "You're right." Then, after hearing the second litigant, he said to him, "You're right." The cleric's exasperated wife, who had been listening to the whole case, said to him, "But they're saying opposing things. They can't both be right," to which the rabbi responded, "You're also right."

❧

Dear Joseph,

I'm a physician who has recently started a highly selective fellowship at a top medical center. While the fellowship is highly sought after, the pay is meager, though it is in line with what this type of fellowship usually pays. When I complete the fellow-ship in five years, my salary could easily rise tenfold. However, in the meantime, because of my low salary, my family of three qualifies for food stamps. Given that our current low income is temporary and we're looking at a huge increase in the future, is it right/

ethical for me to go on the dole at this time by taking food stamps? Does it make a difference that over the course of my life, I will almost certainly pay a lot more in taxes than I will receive in services?

Temporarily Poor

Dear Temporarily Poor,

I happen to have recently been studying a twelfth-century legal text by the Jewish philosopher Moses Maimonides (who, by interesting coincidence, was, like you, also a physician), which discusses an analogous problem. Maimonides rules that if a traveler who has assets at home finds himself without funds on the road, he is permitted to go to a local charity fund and request assistance. When he returns home (and in medieval times, this could have been months later), he has no legal requirement to pay back the money given him by the charity, since at the time he requested the assistance he was in genuine need. In other words, the fact that the traveler will some months later have sufficient funds to support himself doesn't mean that he should refuse assistance when he genuinely needs it.

Similarly, the fact that you will make substantial amounts of money in another five years does nothing to assuage your family's current need for food. So if you receive a small enough salary to qualify for food stamps, I see no moral reason why you should refrain from using them. (An exception would be if your income were being supplemented by substantial gifts from your or your wife's family.)

That you feel a measure of guilt for taking food stamps reflects well on your character, since you realize that food stamps are intended for society's neediest members, and not for medical specialists. However, I believe that down the road you have a moral, though not a legal, obligation to find a way to pay back (I'll give several examples of what I mean later in my answer) the value of the food stamps you have received. Why?

My reasoning is as follows: There is no requirement that you study on this special fellowship. You've already trained as a physician and are capable of working and earning sufficient money so that you need not receive government subsidies. It is only because you have made a personal decision to continue your studies (a decision, I suspect, motivated both by idealism—you want to acquire specialized knowledge that will enable you to help people—and by the desire to make more money in the future) that you have *voluntarily* put yourself in a deprived circumstance and therefore now need government assistance. This is what distinguishes you from most food-stamp recipients, the large majority of whom did not arrive at that state voluntarily.

Therefore, I would suggest the following: Keep a basic tab of how much you receive over the coming year or years, and once you embark on your career, make donations in that amount to charitable organizations such as City Harvest or Food for Survival that provide food directly to people in need. Also, let this whole experience, which I assume from the tone of your letter you find to be somewhat embarrassing, cause you to have greater compassion for those who are involuntarily poor, and make sure that when you do "make it," you treat a certain percentage of your patients who otherwise wouldn't be able to afford your services at very low rates or free of charge.

Dear Joseph,

When I ride the train into work, I often find that the ticket I paid for is not collected. This leaves me free to use the ticket at a later date. I realize that this is a form of stealing, since I'm using the ticket more than once, even though I have paid for only one ride. A hard-and-fast rule would seem to be, Don't use the ticket again and be done with it. In speaking about it with my significant other, however, she pointed out that

- the trains in our area, through ineptitude or accidents, waste a significant portion of our time, so we're simply "getting our own back";
- the excruciatingly high taxes we pay more than make up for any lost revenue incurred by the transit authority;
- if they really wanted our tickets, they'd collect them, and we're not responsible for their lack of responsibility.

I would never dream of stealing from a person standing alongside me, but I often wonder if it's even possible to act in an immoral way toward an entity that only exists as a construct of imagination, and whose corporate actions I would occasionally describe as unethical (e.g., oil companies or lumber companies that abuse the environment). What are your thoughts on this matter?

Ambivalent

Dear Ambivalent,

Your significant other argues that it is okay to cheat the transit authority, because, for example, it's wasted your time on other occasions and you're getting your "own back." But if the fact that the transit authority has wasted your time entitles you to cheat it, then why restrict such cheating to instances in which they accidentally fail to take your ticket? Your partner's reasoning would suggest that it would be okay to steal from the transit authority, if you could, a commuter ticket (indeed, there have been widely publicized instances in New York City of people stealing MetroCards for use on the subway system). What your partner is advocating is merely an instance of rationalizing, which, when you think about it, simply means using your reason to justify what is wrong.

I would offer a similar answer in response to your partner's annoyance about the high taxes you are paying, an annoyance that I share, but that doesn't justify stealing. In addition, cheating the transit authority seems like a pretty indirect and petty way to register such annoyance.

Regarding the transit authority's lack of responsibility in not collecting your tickets, the company might indeed have harried or irresponsible employees. Does that mean you should take advantage of that irresponsibility? And if you do, what does that say about your character?

More significantly, once you conclude that some cheating is right, where will it end? What happens at the supermarket when a clerk accidentally gives you ten dollars more in change than you deserve? Will you reason, "She was careless, and I'm not responsible for her lack of responsibility"? Many people do indeed keep extra money that they have been wrongfully given, but what reveals most such people to be hypocrites is that they do not stay silent when they are accidentally given too little change. Then, they insist that the error be corrected. Would you want to have a person who takes advantage of another's error as your business partner?

Concerning what you wrote about lumber companies that pollute the environment: If indeed you believe that they are wrong to do so, a principled response would be to refuse to use their products. But saying that because you find their behavior immoral on one issue or another you will cheat them sounds suspiciously like a rationalization once again.

Also, you describe companies as entities that only exist "as a construct of imagination." But companies, even huge ones, are real. They have shareholders, and they have employees. If enough people cheat such companies, they will go bankrupt, the employees will lose their jobs, and the shareholders will lose the value of their investments. So much for the argument that you "would never dream of stealing from a person standing alongside" you. Without intending to hurt such a person, such acts of dishonesty will inflict real harm.

Finally, if you and your significant other someday have children, what do you want to teach them? "Hey, look how lucky we are. The conductor forgot to collect our tickets. Now we get to go again for free"? Or, alternatively, "The conductor made a mistake and forgot to take our tickets. Let's tell him, because it's not fair to take advantage of his mistake"? Which lesson do you want to impart?

I strongly suspect that parents who follow the latter course will raise finer children. And I certainly hope that that is something that matters both to you and your significant other.

Dear Joseph,

A friend's elderly mother often forgets why she's living in a nursing home, and wonders where her deceased husband is.

Meanwhile, her oldest daughter, who has power of attorney, asked me to witness her mother's signature on a real-estate transfer of vacation property. She explained that she and her sister want sole ownership of the cottage so that when their mother dies (which is expected to happen soon), they can avoid a cash settlement with an out-of-state brother on this item of the estate.

Knowing that the mother is not capable of making this decision for herself, I refused. But should the brother be told of his sister's plan? Or should the court, which granted power of attorney, know of the proposed misuse of authority? Advice would be appreciated.

In a Quandary over Friendship

Dear In a Quandary over Friendship,

What is quite remarkable is not only that your friend wishes to act in a manner that appears highly dishonest, but also that she is so confident that you will help her do so. I presume that she has worked out in her mind her rationalization for trying to deprive her brother from a part—perhaps a significant part—of their mother's estate. The most likely rationalization is that because she lives near her mother, she feels that she has spent far more time attending to her elderly parent than has her brother, and thus is entitled to a larger share of the estate. Certainly, when some children live far away, the children who live closest to an aging parent feel that the burden has fallen disproportionately on them.

Nonetheless, if the facts are as you have stated, this woman's act is particularly odious. Many people might think that the sole victim of her act is her brother, but there is a second victim as well: her mother. The court designated this sister with a power of attorney to act in the mother's best interests, and to carry out her wishes when she is no longer in a position to do so. However, this woman apparently has decided to act in her own best interests, and against her mother's intentions. This elderly, confused woman was once healthy and mentally focused. Apparently, when well, she intended to divide her estate equally among her children; that, it would seem, is the reason the daughter is now trying to remove this item from the estate. In general, dividing an estate equally among one's offspring is the most moral thing for a parent to do so that the children feel that the parent loved them equally. Presumably, if the mother could understand what was transpiring, she would be heartbroken as well as outraged to know that one or two of her daughters were attempting to dispossess their brother, her son, out of his share of a significant asset in the estate. (Even if the brother has been a derelict son, it would have been up to the mother to craft her will in such a way so as to appropriately benefit the children she wished to favor.)

Clearly, you're in an unpleasant situation. If you feel that you have any chance of succeeding, you should speak to this woman and try to influence her to change her behavior. If that doesn't work, I suggest that you consult a lawyer for advice. My personal instinct is that the brother should be made aware of the existence of this piece of property and that there currently is discussion about ownership of the house and land being transferred, and, perhaps, even of the land being sold (you might do so without revealing your identity—e.g., by sending a letter from a supposed would-be buyer: "We understand that you and/or your mother own a piece of property in . . ."). If you have reason to suspect that the sister is engaging in other acts of fraud to advance her own financial interests, the court that gave her power of attorney should learn that she is abusing that power.

If I have such strong personal instincts in this manner, why then do I suggest that you first consult with a lawyer? Because I recognize that it can be quite dangerous to act in an ethically pure manner in an overly litigious society. A dear friend of mine, a lawyer with whom I consulted about your letter, told me that while it's true that a fiduciary (as is the sister here) should never act in a manner inconsistent with the wishes and desires of the granter of the power, and to the detriment of others in favor of her own interest, he also advised me to warn you that if you convey to the brother (or to the court) that this woman was trying to act in a dishonest manner, she will deny the charge and may well sue you for slander.

A short, final thought: Perhaps the best known of the Ten Commandments is the fifth: "Honor your father and mother." If the facts as you have conveyed them are accurate, then how sad that one of this woman's final acts toward her dying mother is so profound an act of dishonor.

Dear Joseph,

A friend of mine, overwhelmed by his debts, confided to me that he's filed for bankruptcy. I didn't say anything to him, but inside I was feeling that there's something immoral about declaring bankruptcy and thereby freeing yourself from debts you yourself incurred. Am I being unfairly judgmental?

Bankrupt's Uneasy Friend

Dear Bankrupt's Uneasy Friend,

I can't fully answer whether you are being unfairly judgmental, because you haven't provided me with enough information, and whether or not declaring bankruptcy is immoral depends on that information. For example, if your friend borrowed responsibly, spent his money prudently (particularly in the months preceding the bankruptcy), and then, through a series of events that he could not reasonably have anticipated, suffered a great decline in income and assets, then the declaration of bankruptcy would not be immoral.

Still, many bankruptcies in the United States today *do* strike me as immoral, particularly when incurred by people who bought on credit or who borrowed money without a credible plan for repaying their debts.

Particularly immoral is making unnecessary purchases when one is already aware that he or she is in a tight circumstance, and may have to declare bankruptcy. Also immoral are those who incur student loans in order to acquire a higher education and who then declare bankruptcy as they prepare to practice the profession they studied on money borrowed from others.

In short, if a person or a bank or a store sold you something or lent you money and relied on your word that you would pay, you are morally obligated to do so. Thus, it seems to me that even when a declaration of bankruptcy is justified, if one subsequently makes back the money owed, one has a moral (although not a legal) obligation to repay old debts. The Golden Rule of "Do unto others as you would have others do unto you" applies here. If someone purchased something or borrowed money from you, subsequently declared bankruptcy, and became solvent again, wouldn't you want to be repaid?

Dear Joseph,

Recently, I was running across the street at night and tripped over some unmarked construction—a deep pit right in front of the sidewalk. I fell on my face, broke my front tooth, and had numerous lacerations. I went to a nearby hospital emergency room for stitches. I've had to have ongoing dental work to replace the damaged tooth. I feel like suing the city because of the construction, but I feel guilty because if I hadn't been running, the injury probably wouldn't have been as bad. Should I go ahead and sue?

Feeling Both Guilty and Angry

Dear Feeling Both Guilty and Angry,

Sue, with no sense of guilt. The people who should be feeling guilty are the ones who dug the deep pit and left it open and unmarked. That is flagrantly irresponsible, and you can be sure that if they, or a family member, fell into an open, unmarked pit, they would be suing as well. True, you might not have fallen in or hurt yourself as severely if you hadn't been running, but so what? If these other people had not acted so irresponsibly, you wouldn't have been hurt at all. Besides, it could just as easily have been a child who fell in, or a blind person.

I hope you win your suit, because a loud and clear message must be sent that human beings bear responsibility for damage that they should clearly be able to anticipate. Leaving an open pit in an area traversed by people is simply wrong.

My only other advice to you is of a more commonsensical nature: It's better not to run on city streets, particularly at night.

I wish you a speedy and complete recovery.

Dear Joseph,

Last week, I took my thirteen-year-old daughter to the bank to deposit some holiday gifts in her savings account. I noticed when we got home that the bank had erroneously credited her account with an extra $1,000. My daughter is asking if we need to tell the bank of its mistake. I know this seems like a no-brainer; of course we should. But this particular bank charges all kinds of fees for services on my daughter's tiny account for which she gets a measly 2 percent interest. I think it costs her more to keep it there than to keep it under a mattress. Why can't we just wait and see if the bank notices the error?

Slightly Vengeful

Dear Slightly Vengeful,

A friend of mine once withdrew $500 from his bank's ATM machine. Only the cash never came out; all he got was a receipt noting that he had made a $500 withdrawal. He called the bank immediately, using the phone alongside the ATM machine. The bank employee he talked to was totally unsympathetic. She claimed that their records indicated that the cash had been disbursed, and she refused to credit his account for the $500. My friend told me that many angry thoughts went through his head; he swore to himself that he would withdraw all his money from that bank and take it elsewhere. In the end, he concluded that while ideally that was what he should have done, it would have been too inconvenient for him to do so.

There is no question in my mind that if the bank subsequently made a $500 error in his favor, he would have no moral obligation to inform it of the mistake; indeed, I believe he would be acting foolishly if he did so.

So now let's look at your case. You don't claim

that the bank ever took a thousand dollars from your daughter. Rather, you complain that the bank imposes unfair monthly charges on her account, charges that annoy you but that, I suspect, have amounted to far, far less than a thousand dollars (and you did, in any case, agree to open an account there). Therefore, I cannot for the life of me imagine why you should be entitled to such a sum. After all, if a bank error had inadvertently led to a thousand dollars being deducted from your or your daughter's account, you would protest loudly and vigorously. And you'd be particularly outraged if you learned that the bank had known of the error but decided to say nothing unless you brought the matter up. In such a case, you would probably go to the police or a lawyer and get the bank in big trouble for trying to steal from you.

I believe in the principle "Do unto others as you would have others do unto you." Thus, if I would regard a bank's acting in the way I am acting as immoral, then I'm doing something immoral myself. Also, do you really want to teach your daughter to take advantage of banks like this? Will this be a good lesson for her to learn?

I suggest that you go to the highest official you know at your bank and tell him or her about the error. Then ask the official, as a courtesy, to find a way to reduce or eliminate some charges from your daughter's account. Make it clear that you're asking this as a favor; you aren't insisting that the bank is obligated to reward you for being honest. If the bank officer chooses to make some adjustment, good. If he or she doesn't, I would regard such behavior as unfriendly, even boorish, and, if convenient, I would suggest that you remove your daughter's and your own account to another bank. But don't keep money that was given to you by accident. It's not right, and you know it. And most important, you want your daughter to know it, too.

Dear Joseph,

I'm in my late seventies now. My husband died some years ago, and I have two children, a married daughter with three children of her own, and a son who's been divorced twice and who has one son. My will has been drawn so as to give the large majority of my estate to my daughter. I have several reasons for doing so. My daughter is more devoted to me than my son, though he is by no means remiss. More important, her expenses are greater than his. I have a close friend who tells me that she thinks it very unwise to divide my estate in an unequal manner. Shouldn't I have the right to dispose of my money as I see fit?

Set in My Ways

Dear Set in My Ways,

If you're talking about the legal right to dispose of your money as you see fit, you are, of course, right. You could, in fact, choose to disinherit your son and grandson entirely, or both of your children, for that matter. However, there are reasons both commonsen-

sical and moral why it is not usually wise to avail ourselves of all our rights. Such, in fact, is what I believe
in your case.

You mention that you want to give your daughter, and presumably through her, to her children, the
large majority of your estate. Since your son and his
son will undoubtedly learn of this unequal division,
what conclusion do you think they will draw from
your will? I would guess that they will assume that
you loved your daughter and her children more than
you loved them.

I know a man who was one of several sons in a
family that also included one daughter, who seemed
to be the mother's favorite child. At her death, the
mother left this daughter a somewhat larger share
of her estate. As noted, it was only somewhat, not
greatly, larger. But this man has always interpreted his
mother's will as yet another indication of his mother's
greater love for his sister than for him and his brothers. How else could it be regarded? Need I add, the
knowledge has been a source of distress to him.

But what if one child truly has greater expenses,
or a lower income, than the others? Even in such a
case, I would counsel that the fair thing is to divide
the estate evenly. If doing so will truly provoke great
financial hardship, then, at the very least, the parent
should discuss with the child who is going to be given
a smaller share why the parent is dividing the estate
unequally. Only if the child accepts this division as
fair do I believe the parent should go ahead and dispose of his assets unevenly. Why?

First, as I suggested, the child receiving less will feel less loved. Now, it is quite possible that you do love your daughter more than you love your son. But do you really want to make it so clear to him that this is the case? Many parents feel a preference for one child over another, but they usually try not to make this preference known. It is immensely damaging to a person's ego to feel that even one's own father and mother, the two people whose love should automatically be counted on, did not particularly love him or her.

Second, apart from the financial legacy, think of the emotional legacy you are bequeathing to your children. The likelihood that your son will remain close with the daughter who received the larger bequest is slim. For all you know, he might come to harbor great animosity toward her, thinking that she talked you into leaving her more money. In any case, he is apt to feel jealousy. Thus, your act is likely to cause a diminution in family feeling in your children. As a parent, I know how important it is to me that my children grow up to love each other. I would be very loath to take a step that I felt could cause that love to be diminished or shattered.

A further thought: Would your late husband, who presumably is responsible for at least a part of the estate you are now preparing to bequeath, have approved of what you are doing? Or might he have wanted his son and daughter to inherit equally?

Yes, there are instances where a child's very bad behavior would justify disinheriting him or her, or sharply reducing the child's share of the estate. But you note that your son has "by no means" been "remiss." Be careful, therefore, that you, too, don't act in a manner that is emotionally and financially remiss toward him.

Dear Joseph,

In a recent column you argued that parents should always leave their children equal shares in the estate, because any unequal division is likely to lead to one child's feeling less loved, and to bitterness between the siblings. In my family, just the opposite happened. My mother has two cousins, a man and a woman, who have not been on speaking terms with each other because of their father's will. In that case, the father did divide the main part of his estate, a thriving hardware store, equally. However, because the male cousin had worked full-time running the store for many years, he believed he was entitled to own the store outright.

Where There's a Will, There's a Problem

Dear Where There's a Will, There's a Problem,

It seems to me that in this case the father acted unwisely—but not because he divided the estate equally. He had, I believe, a moral obligation to make known to the son that even though the son was running the store full-time, the father still intended to divide the store equally between his two children. The son could then have decided whether or not he wished to continue working in the store, or whether he would prefer to start out on his own.

I'm curious to know how the son came to make the assumption that he was going to be given full ownership of the store. This assumption might well have made sense if he worked there on a volunteer basis, while the sister refused to help out. But if he made his living running the store, then why should he also be the store's sole inheritor? He hadn't started the business. His father, I assume, did, and his father wished his two children to share equally in the estate.

What this case underscores is the importance of parents' discussing inheritance issues with children while the parents are still alive, in order to avoid leaving behind unpleasant emotional legacies. How sad this father would be to learn that his two children don't speak to each other anymore, and what a painful violation of the Fifth Commandment to "Honor your father and mother."

Dear Joseph,

My great-aunt died, leaving her entire estate of $500,000 to me. Unfortunately, she wrote her own will and made a mistake by not having two independent witnesses (she had one). The will was set for a probate hearing, but unexpectedly, unknown distant relatives came out of the woodwork demanding their share. I'm aware that this happens often. The matter is going into mediation, and I'm sick about it. I cared for Rose during the last ten years of her life. We were very close, and she wanted me to benefit from her years of saving and investing. I have been wanting to write to these "vultures," as I refer to them, and try to appeal to some sense of fairness. Isn't it wrong of them to take what is not deserved? Just because the law allows a person to take something, can they not show restraint? What can I say to make them act fairly?

Feeling Cheated

Dear Feeling Cheated,

Unfortunately, if these people truly are the "vultures" which you describe, any letter from you won't influence them. Ironically, only if they're somewhat better people than you credit them as being is there a chance that they'll take to heart an appeal from you. Therefore, I suggest that in writing them, you try to restrain your bitterness. Otherwise, it will seep into your letter and make either no impression or a bad one.

I would suggest you write something like this to them:

As you perhaps know, I spent a great deal of time with Great-aunt Rose during the last decade of her life, and took care of her and her affairs. We became very close during this time, and she made it known to me that since she had no other close relatives, and since I was the only relative who was caring for her, it was her intention to bequeath to me her entire estate. And indeed she did so bequeath, except that she made a legal mistake (one witness, instead of two). But her desire was known to her, to me, and now to you. I therefore appeal to your consciences to allow her final bequest to be disbursed as she wished. I am sure that in comparable circumstances (e.g., you had been the sole relative helping a sick relative, and there had been a legal mix-up) you would wish the same to occur.

Yet, even if the letter makes some impact, I doubt that your relatives will back off completely. Therefore, make a settlement if you can. From my experience with disputes over money, it's almost always worth compromising. Otherwise, even if you are morally in the right, the main victim of the feeling of injustice will be you, and the sense of ongoing bitterness against the people you refer to as vultures will have a detrimental effect on the quality of your life. Once a settlement is made, you are likely to think about the injustice much less. And that will be good for your soul.

Dear Joseph,
Recently, my fiancé's mother died (his father died several years ago), and she divided her estate

evenly between her two children, my fiancé and his sister. His sister has three children, and she now insists that she and her family should receive significantly more than half—perhaps three-quarters—of the estate, since it is unfair that her children not share in the inheritance. She acknowledges that while the law may be on my fiancé's side, his action in keeping half of the estate is immoral. Her increasingly strident harangues on the subject have thrown him into a depression. She's made it clear that if he doesn't give in on this issue, any further relationship between them will be pointless since "that will show that all you care about is money." Should my fiancé compromise and give his sister and her children part of his share of the estate?

Confused

Dear Confused,

Normally, I am a big advocate of compromise, especially when it comes to maintaining good family relations. And maybe if it were possible to buy real peace with his sister with a token settlement I would suggest doing so. But in all honesty I find your fiancé's sister's reasoning to be so self-serving as to be immoral. For one thing, it was the deceased mother who divided the estate between her two children (it would have been wise and right for her to leave some special gift to each grandchild), and now her daughter wants to thwart her dead mother's will. Doing so, especially given what seems to me the mother's fair will, strikes me as very wrong.

The sister's self-serving nature seems apparent to me in yet another way. I somehow doubt that if you and your fiancé were to marry tomorrow and in another year have quadruplets, she would argue that the estate should be reconfigured so that your fiancé and your children receive the larger share. Instead, she would probably come up with another argument, such as "Well, the estate should only go to those grandchildren whom Grandma knew personally."

Your fiancé's sister undoubtedly insists that her reasoning is not selfish but merely a statement of the right thing to do. Therefore, let her brother suggest that she solve this dilemma in the next generation. She can start now by informing her three children that when they grow up, if one of them does not marry or is infertile, he or she will receive a smaller share in the estate than those siblings who do have children. She can further increase family harmony by making it known that the child who has the most children will receive the most money.

I hope it's obvious that I don't want her to follow my advice, since by doing so, all that will happen is that this woman will destroy her children's love for one another, as she is now undermining whatever love exists between her brother and herself. Had the grandmother had real insight into the character of this daughter, perhaps she could have sidestepped the issue by leaving half of her estate directly to her grandchildren.

Tell your fiancé that he has no reason to feel

guilty. And while I understand his sorrow at the deterioration in his relationship with his sister—the only other surviving member of his original nuclear family—any peace he achieves with her through concessions probably will be illusory and transient. Selfish people are rarely, if ever, satisfied with what they have, so even if he were to buy peace with her now, her selfishness may manifest itself again in the future. Unfortunately—and I know no way to avoid this—she will probably spend the next ten years or so poisoning her children's minds against their uncle. It seems to me that for the foreseeable future your fiancé's best hope for having a family may be to make one with you. God willing, at some time in the future, his sister may change her attitude or at least stop being preoccupied with this issue, and he will then be able to reestablish a relationship with her.

Postscript: Every letter I received supported the brother in this ugly fight, but one reader seemed to nail the sister's character with great precision: "I find it interesting that the sister says that if the brother doesn't yield, all he is interested in is money. I wonder if she considers that if she doesn't yield, all she is interested in is money."

This comment reminded me of an old rabbinic proverb: "A character flaw that you have, don't go about attributing to others."

Dear Joseph,

A close friend who became wealthy during the stock-market run-up of the late 1990s has lost just about everything. He's told me a few times how guilty he feels toward his family, and that he would be better off dead so that at least his wife and children would have the one substantial asset he has left: his life-insurance policy. Alarmed by the direction of his thinking, I pointed out that insurance companies don't pay off on policies when someone commits suicide. But he told me that as long as one has held the policy for at least two years, companies are required to pay. I don't think he's really going to kill himself, but I would appreciate any arguments you can think of that might dissuade him.

Feeling Responsible

Dear Feeling Responsible,

In the aftermath of the 1929 stock-market crash, a despondent investor, in a situation remarkably similar to that of your friend, approached Rabbi Stephen S. Wise. The man told the rabbi that since his life-insurance policy was the sole asset he could still leave his family, he wanted to know if it was okay for him to kill himself.

Rabbi Wise told the man to go to his wife and children and tell them what he was planning to do. If they told him that they would prefer that he not commit suicide, then he had a clear answer: They wanted him alive, even if that left them poor. But if they told him that they would prefer the life-insurance money, then, Rabbi Wise asked him, "Are you going to kill yourself for the sake of selfish people like that?"

I would tell your friend to follow the same advice. I would also remind him, forcefully, that life can be meaningful and worthwhile, even if one is poor. Throughout history, most people have been poor, and there is no reason to think that they derived no enjoyment from their lives because of that. Poor people are as capable as wealthy people of being in love with their spouses and having loving relationships with their children, blessings that can bring people more joy than money (indeed, there is no shortage of wealthy people who commit suicide, precisely because they lack such relationships). Life may be harder without money, but if the only thing that made your friend's life worthwhile until now was his wealth, then his life was worthless even before he lost his money.

I would also urge the man to see a doctor or a psychiatrist, either of whom could evaluate whether he needs to be hospitalized, receive medication, or be in therapy. In addition, I would also tell the man's wife that he is feeling very despondent and that she should do what she can to assuage his sense of guilt for having brought poverty upon his family. She also could play a role in helping him to get professional help.

Dear Joseph,

There's a famous teaching in the talmudic book the Ethics of the Fathers, "If I am not for myself, who will be for me?" In line with this dictum, I give all my charity to Jewish causes; after all, if Jews don't support Jewish charitable needs, who will? My wife thinks I'm wrong, that I owe it to the society in which I live to spread around my giving. But I don't think there's anything wrong with what I'm doing. Is there?

Generous to a Fault?

Dear Generous to a Fault?,

You quoted only the first part of the talmudic citation, which then continues, "But if I am only for myself, what am I?" Just as it's wrong to ignore your own religious community's needs, so, too, is it wrong to ignore the needs of the broader community of which you also are a part. Also, it's not always easy to determine what is Jewish charitable giving and what isn't. Is medical research—for example, finding a cure for cancer—a non-Jewish issue, and supporting a Jewish school a Jewish one? Or are they both issues of concern to the Jewish community and therefore both issues you should support? And, perhaps you are not aware that the Talmud—the very religious source on which you base your attitude to support only Jewish causes—mandates that Jews support non-Jewish as well as Jewish poor.

Having said that, I would like to add that I

believe it is appropriate for members of any religious or ethnic group to donate a disproportionate percentage of their charity to causes that serve their community, both because such causes matter so much to them and because their community depends on its members for support. Jews, for example, comprise only about 2 percent of the American population and, as you aptly note, if they don't support Jewish causes, who will?

Also, I would argue that a person who gives most of his charity to his own religious or ethnic community is still, *in effect,* supporting charitable causes outside his community, as long as he also pays taxes. That's because today the government has taken over many of the functions once performed by charitable groups—such as welfare payments to the poor. The fact that a significant percentage of our taxes is used to support those in need should liberate us from feeling guilty about giving a large percentage to our own religious, racial, or ethnic community.

But don't give all your donations to your own community. It's not good for your character. If you do that long enough, you'll stop seeing everyone as being equally created in God's image, and therefore worthy of your help. We are, after all, all members of one race, the human race.

Dear Joseph,

For several years, I've been tithing, giving away 10 percent of my income each year to charity. Should I base the tithe, though, on gross income or after-tax income?

Tither

Dear Tither,

Money that you pay in taxes is not yours; in effect, it belongs to the government, and every April 15, you're required to turn it over to "Uncle Sam." So it seems to me that it would be unfair to burden a person with having to give away 10 percent of money he or she will not keep, and may never even see (i.e., if it's deducted directly from your paycheck).

The injustice of asking a person to base his or her tithe on gross, and not net, income can be illustrated by going back to the 1950s, a time when the marginal tax rates in the United States were as high as 90 percent. Can you imagine telling a person that he owed 90 percent of the highest portion of his income in taxes, and the remaining 10 percent to charity?

In short, what you don't keep, you shouldn't have to tithe. The fact that you tithe based on net income is in itself uncommon, and very commendable. Congratulations!

Dear Joseph,

My husband and I bought an apartment for investment purposes and placed it with a broker. A couple came to look at the apartment, liked it, and told our broker that they accepted the $4,000-a-month rent that we had requested. We were pleased, but the broker insisted that he should still show the apartment to a few other people, since there's always a chance that the first couple might renege on their commitment.

The following day, another couple saw the apartment, loved it, and offered to pay $4,500 a month. The broker is advising us to take the second offer, since our agreement with the first couple was only verbal. But what do you think—am I obligated to stay with my original commitment, or should I accept the second offer, which amounts to an extra $6,000 a year, money we could really use?

Perplexed

Dear Perplexed,

You put something on the market at a price that you yourself specified. Someone agreed to the price, and you accepted their offer. Are you bound by this agreement or not?

If you are asking a legal question, the answer is obvious. Because nothing was signed, you're not legally bound to abide by your commitment. If you are asking me a moral question, the answer is very different. It seems to me that it would be immoral for you to back out of this deal. The people who made the first bid relied on your word and accepted the conditions you laid down. To paraphrase Samuel Goldwyn, we are living in a pretty sad world if verbal agreements are not worth the paper on which they are not written.

As a practical matter, I would notify the people whose offer you accepted that you have been made another, higher, offer, and therefore, in addition to their verbal commitment to rent your apartment, you wish them to immediately (let's say over a forty-eight-hour period) sign a lease. If they refuse to sign right away, then you have the moral right to enter into an agreement with the second couple. By making such a notification, you will be doing the fair thing while also protecting your own interests.

Dear Joseph,

For thirty-three years, I was a taxi driver in New York. I used to hang out at JFK Airport, and bring a lot of foreign visitors into the city. But instead of charging them what was on the meter, I charged them pretty much whatever I could get away with. I never got caught, but I'm seventy-four now, not in the best of health, and I feel very bad about what I did. I've only talked about this with my wife, and she feels I'm making a big mountain out of a molehill. But I really would like to figure out some way to undo what I've done. But anytime I try to think through what I can do, I come up with zilch.

Repentant in Queens

Dear Repentant in Queens,

Repentance depends in large measure on undoing the evil act you have committed. For example, let's say that I cheat you out of a thousand dollars and regret what I have done. The most necessary step in my repentance is to return the money to you and seek your forgiveness. Even if I'm not in a position to repay you, I can still seek your forgiveness, and you might choose to say, "I forgive you, and don't worry about the money."

Unfortunately, as touched as I am by the obvious sincerity of your repentance, you have committed one of those sins for which it is now impossible to undo the damage done. When one defrauds the public, whether it be through the sort of deception in which you engaged as a taxi driver, or through a pyramid scheme or stock-market manipulation, there's not a whole lot one can do. Because you don't know the names of your victims, you are not in a position either to return the money or to request forgiveness.

In the words of a two-thousand-year-old legal text known as the *Tosefta*, Jewish ethics advises those who have defrauded the public to "pay back those whom they know they defrauded and to devote the balance to public needs." In ancient times, this might have meant digging a well that could service the public.

Today, you could perhaps contribute to a park, library, hospital, or something else that benefits the entire community. You mention that the victims of your behavior were foreigners. If, for example, you cheated many Japanese tourists, you might make these donations to a park, library, or hospital in Japan, thereby benefiting people in the country whose citizens you defrauded. Alternatively, if no one country seems appropriate, make a gift to an organization such as Travelers Aid.

A Question for Which I Have No
Fully Satisfactory Answer

Dear Joseph,
Should charities refuse to accept contributions from donors who acquired their money in an immoral manner?
A Proponent of Moral Giving

Dear Proponent of Moral Giving,
If you're collecting money for an organization that is helping people in need, you can end up hurting a lot of needy people if you become too picky about whose money you choose to accept. For example, consider one of America's premier philanthropists, Andrew Carnegie, a man who, a century ago, donated tens of millions of dollars (the equivalent in

today's terms of perhaps a billion dollars or more) to build libraries and greatly expand universities.

Yet Carnegie also was the owner of the steel company whose workers in Homestead, Pennsylvania, went on strike in 1892 to protest, among other things, having to work twelve hours a day, seven days a week.

Do I regard such an employment policy as immoral? Yes, and it also violated a code most Americans regard as the pillar of ethics, the Ten Commandments, which requires you to give those whom you employ—and even the animals that work for you—one day a week off (see Exodus 20:10).

Should Carnegie's contributions, therefore, have been rejected? No, because I believe it was in society's broader interests to allow him to do good. Otherwise, society would place itself in the self-destructive position of permitting a wealthy businessman to do many bad things (as long as he technically violated no law), while refusing to profit from his philanthropic activities.

What if the money is donated by someone who acquired it illegally?

Some years ago, a major Jewish seminary received a $2 million donation from a man who, it was subsequently revealed, had acquired much of his wealth through insider trading (he had bribed employees of companies to reveal to him confidential information about upcoming mergers). The organization did not return the money, arguing, as I recall, that they had already spent it and that it would be difficult, if not impossible, to raise new money to replace these funds.

They did, however, refuse to name their library for the now imprisoned felon (as they had earlier promised to do), an act with which I concurred for two reasons. First, it would be incongruous, to say the least, to name a building for a man whose name had become a byword for stock-market deceit. Second, since the man acquired much of his wealth through deceit, one could argue that much of what he donated, in effect, belonged to other people. If anything, those people, not he, were entitled to have the building named for them (what they were really entitled to was to get their money back, but there was no reason to assume that the money donated to the Jewish seminary was precisely the money stolen from them; after all, some of this man's assets were acquired honestly).

So while, in theory, I do believe that organizations should turn down immorally gotten gains, I find that I can't come up with a consistent principle as to when such gifts should be refused and when accepted.

Dear Joseph,

My friend received a call from his landlady last week saying she had recently found the rent check he had sent her (on time, by the way) for last February, nearly a year ago now. The landlady had obviously overlooked or misplaced the check, and never cashed it. My friend's feeling is "Too bad. You had your chance; I paid last February's rent in good faith and on time. You're the one who screwed up, so it's your loss." Obviously, the landlady wants him to write a new check for last February's rent, since the bank won't honor checks after six months. My friend is in a financial bind at the moment (he is obviously not the kind who balances his checkbook on a regular basis), and this would create a hardship. So, is this the landlady's fault and should she just let it go, or should my friend have to repay last February's rent?

Friend of the Victim

Dear Friend of the Victim,

By one of those odd circumstances that one can label coincidence, fate, or destiny, about an hour after I read your letter, I was rummaging through some papers looking for lecture notes for a speech when I came across an eight-month-old receipt for which I have never been reimbursed. A company for which I had done some work had told me to lay out the money and send them a receipt. I had forgotten to do so, misplaced the receipt, and subsequently forgotten about the whole matter. Now that I have the receipt, I am certainly intending to send it along and request reimbursement. Were the company to say to me a variation on what your friend wants to say to his landlady—"Too bad. You had your chance. We told you eight months ago to send in your expenses; now too much time has passed, and it's you who screwed up, so it's your loss"—I would be very upset and think the company dishonest.

We are dealing here with a simple case of an honest mistake, and to take advantage of another's honest mistake is not honest. In addition, you should point out to your friend that he is laboring under a misconception, which is further fueling his sense of victimization. His belief that he paid last February's rent and that he will now have to "repay" it is an error. Though he did send in a check a year ago, since it was never cashed, he did *not* pay last February's rent (even though he intended to do so). Therefore, if he pays now, he will be paying that rent for the first time; he will definitely not be *re*paying it.

Other than learning that it might be wise to start balancing his checkbook, I would suggest that your friend tell his landlady that because of some checkbook miscalculations he is now overdrawn on his account and, having waited a full year for this rent, could she please give him one more month's extension, or if he needs more time, let him pay it in the form of installments? I hope she will comply. On the other hand, if he tries to contest the matter legally, I suspect he will lose, and generate significant, and justified, animosity on his landlady's part. People— landladies and your friend alike—understandably resent another who tries to take advantage of a mistake they made.

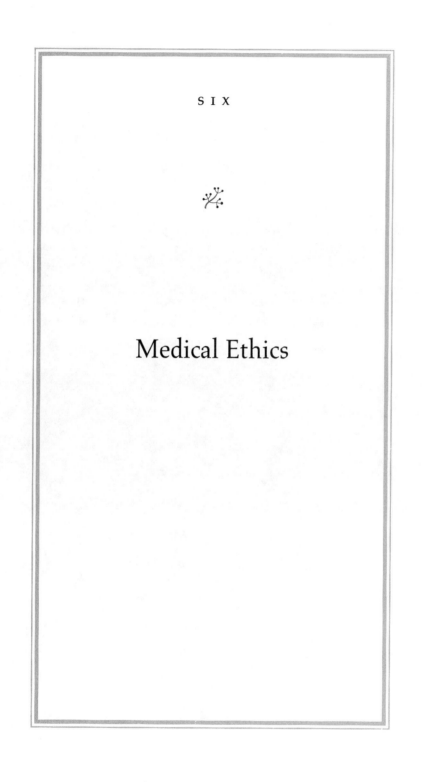

SIX

Medical Ethics

Dear Joseph,

As I'm sure you realize, the waiting list for kidney transplants is long, but people keep telling me that if I go to China, I can receive a kidney quickly. The source of these kidneys, as is well known, is from the bodies of people executed for capital crimes. Is there anything wrong—I admit that the thought makes me queasy—with saving my life by using the organ of someone who committed a heinous offense and was punished for doing so?

Confused

Dear Confused,

An old proverb teaches, "When you sleep with dogs, you wake up with fleas." Many years ago, the United States decided to recognize the authoritarian/ totalitarian Communist regime of China, and has since gone on to pursue an active trade policy with China. When you become increasingly friendly with a government that, among other things, does not believe in the sanctity of human life, it becomes almost inevitable that you start to condone some of that government's evil policies. The increasingly common practice of Americans and other non-Chinese sharing in the harvesting of organs taken from executed Chinese is the latest, most extreme, example of acquiescing to evil. China executes thousands of people each year, far more than any other country in the world. And, because of the speed with which people are arrested, tried, and executed in China, there is compelling reason to believe that a significant percentage of those executed are innocent. Unlike in the United States, in China people are put to death for crimes such as robbery, which, in civilized societies, are not regarded as crimes for which human beings should ever be put to death. Thus, it is reasonable to believe that if you receive a kidney in China, you might be profiting from the death of an innocent human being or one who had committed an offense for which she should not have been executed (even if one is pro–capital punishment for premeditated murderers). In addition, there is a good chance that the organ will come from someone who either did not consent to donate his organ or whose consent was coerced.

Some time ago, the *New York Times* reported on the moral dilemma facing American doctors who are approached by people who received organs in China and who now wish to receive postoperative care in the United States. One doctor argued that he thought it ethically unjust for him to "punish" a patient by withholding treatment just because he, the doctor, thought it wrong to accept a transplant from an executed Chinese prisoner.

The justification offered by this doctor for treating such patients strikes me as ethically problematic. What, after all, are the implications of his argument that since such people are in need of medical care, we have no right to punish them by withholding it? Does that mean that if someone murdered a person in the United States, and then sold the victim's organs to people who knew how they had been procured, the recipients should still be entitled to receive post-transplant treatment from physicians?

What a morally wrongheaded approach! Rather, the U.S. medical community should declare that China's policy of carrying out wide-scale executions and making the organs of executed prisoners available for transplants is immoral. It should stipulate that anyone who chooses to receive such an organ is disqualified from receiving subsequent medical treatment for the transplanted organ in the United States. In the absence of such a declaration, the Chinese leadership will be encouraged to execute more people; for them this is a growth industry, and a highly profitable one at that.

I acknowledge that there's a "crap shoot" here, that among those executed in China undoubtedly are some people who have done terrible things and who may well have deserved to die. But innocent people are also being killed, and there is reason to believe the number is significant. I know my advice will not be easy to follow. But what else can I say, that it's acceptable to profit from what may well be an act of murder? I don't believe that, and in your heart, I hope you don't believe that, either. All we can hope for is that we can influence more Americans to donate their organs when they die [see the next letter for a suggestion as to how we can do so].

Dear Joseph,

Right now, there's an enormous shortage of organs available for transplants. In consequence, as long as a suitable match is found, organs are assigned on a first-come, first-served basis, and there is no way you can be pushed to the top of the list, unless you are near death. Something seems wrong with this system. I read that there was a great delay before Erma Bombeck, the great comic writer and definitely a national asset, was given a kidney transplant (and she died almost immediately thereafter). Shouldn't such a woman have been pushed to the top of the list?

Puzzled and Angry

Dear Puzzled and Angry,

Determining who should live and who should die on the basis of a person's fame or intellectual contribution to society is very tempting—particularly to people who earn their living through their intellect—but it is not moral. Because I believe that human beings are created in God's image, I can't credit the idea that some people are more in God's image than others. Even though I would prefer to see those who committed violent crimes moved to the bottom of the list, I'm aware that horrible moral dilemmas would be unleashed if we awarded transplants on the basis of whose life some committee perceived to be more worthwhile. Think about age differentials: for example, let's compare a sixty-year-old philanthropist with a ten-year-old child. Many people would argue that the child should receive a transplant first, because so much of her life lies before her. But another could counter that the sixty-year-old has already proven himself to be a fine human being, whereas we have no such assurances about the ten-year-old. Or imagine trying to decide between two ten-year-olds on criteria other than greater need and first come, first served. What criteria of character would you use? What questions would you ask the two children, and what questions would you ask others about them? And even if you could come up with good questions, how would you know if you were getting accurate answers? It therefore seems to me that as long as we have an inadequate number of organs available for transplant, the current system probably makes sense.*

There is one exception, however, that I think would benefit humanity, since it would greatly

---

*By the way, the rumor that Mickey Mantle was given preference in getting a liver transplant because he was a celebrity was untrue. Mantle was rushed to the head of the list because he was the most ill person in his region—he was near death—on the day he got his transplant.

increase the number of available organs. I suggest that those who volunteer to donate their undiseased organs after they die be moved to the head of the list. If people knew that being a registered donor would greatly increase the likelihood of their receiving an organ if needed, I think we would see a great increase in the number of people making their organs available. This, in turn, would lead to a far larger percentage of patients receiving needed transplants.

I have, however, encountered one objection to this proposal. Wouldn't it discriminate against those who, for religious reasons, are opposed to donating organs? Yes, but it strikes me as fair that those who oppose giving organs should be at the bottom of the list, not the top, when it comes to getting them.

The good news, however, is that this suggestion might lead to such an increase in the number of available organs that everybody who needs an organ would get one.

Postscript: Normally, when I write a response, I can anticipate the sort of objections my position probably will provoke, but not always. Though I'd never have guessed it, one reader saw my proposal as undermining human virtue:

"If those who are committed to donating an organ in the event of an accident are given preferential treatment if they themselves need it, it would establish an interesting principle: Those who are generous should benefit most. But doesn't that undermine the point of generosity—i.e., to do it selflessly? If you're doing it for a reward, doesn't that make it less generous?"

The main point of generosity, in my view, is not that you do it selflessly, but that good be accomplished. Thus, if rewarding those who offer to donate their organs leads to more organs being donated, and more lives being saved, this alone would justify giving organ donors priority. Ironically, if this proposal is instituted, there are likely to be organs available even for those who have not volunteered to donate their organs.

Dear Joseph,

As a health professional, I have two children in my care, one with a heart condition treatable by organ transplantation, the other terminally ill. How should I approach the parents of the terminally ill child to suggest the possible donation of a heart for the other's treatment? By law, is a health professional obligated to state the case on behalf of the child who can be saved by transplantation to the parents of the terminally ill child?

Concerned Health Professional

Dear Concerned Health Professional,

I'm no expert on law, but as far as the moral issues are concerned, it seems appropriate to discuss with parents of a terminally ill child the possibility of organ donation. What's involved, however, is sensitivity. Have the parents accepted the child's condition? If they haven't, I wouldn't say anything. But you might counter, "Shouldn't I speak up right away because another child's life is at stake?"

I would answer no, for two reasons. First, organs such as hearts are not usually donated to a specified recipient. Medical committees determine who is the person most in need of, and most appropriate to receive, the heart. Second, since it would be forbidden to hasten the death of a terminally ill person to procure a heart for another, you have time to speak to the parents. In fact, they may accept the child's terminal condition only shortly prior to his death. Therefore, whether you secure their consent weeks before or during the final days of their child's life, that won't affect a potential recipient of the child's heart. Obviously, however, if the parents have accepted the terminal nature of their child's illness earlier, it would be good to discuss the possibility of an organ transplantation with them now.

Dear Joseph,

My religion teaches that abortion is murder, and in my heart I agree. I believe that life begins at the moment of conception and that eliminating a fetus is the same as eliminating any other life. Yet part of me hesitates when it comes to rape—I have a gut feeling that a rape victim should have the right to terminate her pregnancy. But, to be logically consistent, murder is murder. How can I reconcile these feelings?

Confused

Dear Confused,

As long as you regard abortion as murder, you indeed have boxed yourself into a position that will forbid a raped woman from having an abortion. Sympathetic as you might be to her plight, you would ask, Why should the fact of her having been violated entitle her to "murder" the fetus?

My view is shaped by the Jewish tradition, which, while strongly limiting instances in which it regards abortion as permissible (e.g., when the mother's physical or mental well-being are imperiled), categorically rejects the notion of abortion as murder. The classic case in Jewish law is one discussed in the Torah. Exodus 21:22–23 rules that if two men are fighting and one murders the pregnant wife of the other, the killer is executed. But if instead of killing the wife, he wounds her and causes her pregnancy to be aborted, "the assailant shall be fined." As this passage makes clear, whatever value the fetus has, the Hebrew Bible (which Christians call the Old Testament) doesn't grant it the status of human life. If it did, the punishment for killing the fetus wouldn't be a monetary fine, but the same as that for killing the woman, i.e., death. Therefore, according to the Hebrew Bible, abortion is definitely not murder.*

I believe that endangerment of the mother's mental well-being should be an important consideration in determining whether or not she should abort. In the

---

*I believe this reasoning corresponds with human experience. Thus, most parents are devastated, often for their entire lifetimes, if one of their children dies. And while it is true that couples suffer great anguish when the woman miscarries, I have never heard of an instance in which the anguish suffered from this tragedy was the same as when a child died.

case of rape, it seems very cruel to force a woman to carry in her body the seed of the man who violated her, and who might well be the person she, justifiably, most hates in the world. A nineteenth-century rabbi, Yehuda Perilman, ruled that a raped woman has the right to abort because a woman differs from "mother earth" in that she need not nurture a seed planted within her against her will; indeed, she may "uproot" a seed illegally sown. I find the rabbi's reasoning persuasive.

If you regard abortion as murder, then of course your reasoning forces you to conclude that a woman who has been violated must bear her violator's child. But if that strikes you as inhuman, then maybe it's worth reconsidering your position. Perhaps you should expand your perspective and conclude that there are times when abortion is a necessary evil.

The Ethics of Stem-Cell Research

The following is my response to a question posed to me by Paul O'Donnell, my editor at Beliefnet.com: Do you regard stem-cell research, which relies on cells taken from fertilized eggs, to be moral?

There are two sides to every question, Lord Herbert Samuel pointed out almost a century ago, because when there

---

Similarly, when a woman miscarries late in a pregnancy, the parents don't hold a funeral service. As social philosopher and political conservative Robert Nisbet has noted, "[T]here is no record of any religion, including Christianity, ever pronouncing an accidental miscarriage as a death to be commemorated in prayer and ritual" (*Prejudices*, p. 1).

are no longer two sides, the question ceases to be a question. Recently, various positions have been forming around the question of stem-cell research. In November 1998, scientists at the University of Wisconsin and Johns Hopkins University found that research using human embryos with cells in the earliest stages of development might lead to cures for such diverse devastating diseases as Alzheimer's, Parkinson's, and diabetes.

Embryonic stem cells are available because of a comparatively new phenomenon—doctors' ability to fertilize an egg outside the uterus. For many couples, such fertilization is their one hope for conceiving a child. And because most fertilized eggs, once implanted into the woman's uterus, will not "take," far more eggs are fertilized than are needed for conception. Thus, once the woman becomes pregnant (perhaps several times), the remaining eggs are almost always destroyed. But until that point, the eggs are stored. An estimated one hundred thousand such fertilized eggs are currently in fertility-clinic freezers.

Opponents argue that these eggs are the biological, and therefore moral, equivalent of human beings. Thus, to them, stem-cell research amounts to medical experimentation on, and ultimately the murder of, human beings. If true, then such experimentation would be truly immoral, no matter how many people's lives could be saved. One doesn't murder some innocent people to save the lives of other innocent people.*

---

*Even in discussions of what constitutes "just war," the death of innocents is only justified when such deaths are the unintended but inevitable by-product of a justifiable military action—e.g., when bombing a legitimate military target results in some innocent people dying. However, "just war"

But if fertilized eggs are truly the equivalent of human life, then why hasn't there been a similar hue and cry over these past years at the discarding of such eggs? Because as Connie Mack, the former Florida senator and pro-life activist, argues, "as long as the fertilized egg is not destined to be placed in a uterus, it cannot become life."

In the course of this increasingly impassioned and bitter debate, a great irony has emerged: The pro-life lobby seems to be taking an antilife position: defending the rights of a fertilized egg that will *never* become human, while denying to sufferers of terrible diseases a significant possibility of being cured from their ailments.

I believe that equating a fertilized egg that will never become human with a human life is an act of personal faith, not of reason. While people have a right to accept theological premises that don't seem reasonable to someone outside their faith, such people shouldn't compel others to accept the policy implications of their faith. For example, I don't expect others to accept my belief that God chose my ancient Israelite ancestors to make Himself known to the world.

Perhaps a more pertinent parallel comes from the Catholic tradition. In 1215, the Fourth Lateran Council accepted as official dogma the doctrine of transubstantiation, which asserted that the wafer used at Mass is miraculously transformed into the body of Jesus. Thus, the wafer is to be regarded not as a symbolic representation of Jesus, but rather as his actual body. Just how literally Catholics

---

doctrines would not permit intentionally killing innocent people as an end in itself, even if the goal were the shortening of the war, and thus saving other innocents' lives.

accepted this teaching is exemplified in the writings of a leading preacher of the thirteenth century, Berthold of Regensburg. He explained that Christ, though present in the wafer, doesn't allow himself to be seen in it, for "who would like to bite off the little head, or the little hands, or the little feet of a little child?"

Obviously, for Catholics who believe in the doctrine of transubstantiation, the wafer truly is the body of Jesus. But this is a theological dogma, not one that it is reasonable to expect non-Catholics to accept—otherwise, we'd all be Catholics. The same applies, I would argue, to equating a fertilized egg with a life. People have no right to insist that others be bound by their theological, as opposed to rationally argued, premises, particularly when human lives and human suffering might be at stake.

If indeed, one day, stem-cell research does bring about cures for some of these terrible diseases, opponents of this research can show their disapproval by refusing to permit themselves to be cured through reliance on what they regard as immoral medical procedures. That will be their choice, and an idealistic one. But to deny others who see their arguments as wrongheaded the possibility of such cures strikes me as wrong on both intellectual and moral grounds.

⚘

Dear Joseph,

I am a fifty-seven-year-old man. My mother recently died after a three-year decline into the hell of

Alzheimer's. By the end, she was reduced to an animal state. It was the worst horror I ever witnessed in my life. My father is eighty-three years old and in good physical health. He has begged me to promise him that I will take his life rather than let him descend into Alzheimer's. I love my father dearly. He is an extraordinary man who stood by my mother until the very end when there were no longer any traces of humanity in her.

This is not a theoretical problem. Although I am not a physician, I can see in my father some of the same early warning signs I noted in my mother. His short-term memory is starting to erode. He has trouble reading. Yet his body is remarkably healthy; I am sure it will outlive his mind.

I have not made the promise he wishes. I am repulsed by the idea of taking any life, let alone my dad's. I also do not wish to bring upon myself and my loved ones the consequences that taking a life might have, both legally and financially. In my distress, I've even fantasized a *Strangers on a Train* scenario, in which I would take the life of someone else's loved one if they were to return the favor. But this does not square with my refusal to take another's life.

On the other hand, I would want the same for myself. If I could not do it myself, I would want someone to terminate my life before what makes me who I am is obliterated.

What do I tell my father? I cannot imagine letting him go through what my mother suffered, or rather, what all of those who loved her suffered after my mother was gone, but some soulless zombie inhabited her corpse. But I cannot imagine being the agent of his death. Time is running out. On top of everything else, I am afraid that my refusal to make this promise might lead him to take his own life prematurely. What do I do?

Very Sad

Dear Very Sad,

Your father wants you to do for him what he couldn't do for his wife, your mother. And why couldn't he kill your mother? Probably for the same reason that you believe you won't be able to put him to death. You are repulsed by the idea of taking any life, let alone your father's.

Needless to say, the situation you describe is awful. And throughout history, I am sure that there have been parents who have made such requests of their children, and some children (I would guess very few) who have complied. But, as you note, you "cannot imagine being the agent of his death." The guilt you might well feel would be something you would have to live with for the rest of your life. And as much as you emphasize the horror of the last years of your mother's life, you do not mention that you walk around now consumed by guilt for not having ended her life. Also, if you follow your father's request, you will be committing a crime. And not a minor one either. Therefore, you will have to keep the manner of your father's death a secret, which is not always easy to do. Further, if what you did becomes known, many people will be skeptical of your motives. For example, did you choose to end your father's life while there was still some money left in his estate, money that you would then inherit? I am not saying that this would be a factor in your making the decision to end your father' s life, but such speculation would do great damage to your name; in addition, you might well incur criminal prosecution.

I do believe that you should validate whatever aspects of your father's wishes that you can. Modern medicine often pressures patients (and their families) to take many measures to prolong life, even when the life that is being prolonged will be one without dignity or pleasure. I see no reason to subject a person to such a prolongation of life (which strikes me as akin to using extraordinary means to keep a convicted felon alive just so that he's healthy enough to be executed), particularly when the person has expressly stated, as has your father, that he does not want his life prolonged. Therefore, honor whatever aspects of your father's desires that you can. For example, your father is just the sort of person for whom a "Do not resuscitate" order would be appropriate. This is what seems right to me, though I hasten to add that the dominant tendency in the Jewish tradition—and I am a rabbi—is almost always to prolong life and to think more in terms of quantity of life than of quality. On the other hand, the Talmud is filled with stories of people who had incurable ailments, and the rabbis prayed to God to show them mercy (i.e., to let them die). Also, I would suggest that while your father still has most of his wits about him, he execute a living will outlining precisely the sort of procedures he does not want done. For example, "If I should be in an incurable or irreversible mental or physical condition with no reasonable expectation of recovery, I direct my attending physician to withhold and withdraw treatment that serves only to prolong my dying." The understanding, as outlined in the living will, would be that treatment would be limited to measures to keep your father comfortable and to relieve pain. With such a document in hand, even if physicians try to convince you to do things your father would not want done, you will find it easier to refuse them.

And what about the risk that your father will commit suicide? It does not seem to me that you can violate your own spirit and tell your father, "Don't worry, Dad, I'll kill you when the time seems appropriate," just to forestall the possibility of his committing suicide now. A parent must understand that to lay upon his children the burden of killing them when the parent's life no longer seems worth living is simply an unfair demand. What you can and should tell your father is, "Dad, you're the one who gave me life, and you can't ask me to take away yours. But let me tell you what I can do for you. Because I love you, I will be here for you throughout your illness, and treat you with the love and compassion you have shown me. Also, I promise you that I will not allow any procedures to be performed on you, or any medications administered to you, except those that will relieve pain. I will not allow your life to be artificially extended."

Your situation is so difficult and so sad that I hope I have not said anything that will make it sadder or harder. All I can offer in addition to my advice is my heartfelt prayer that God shows your father mercy.

SEVEN

Everyday Dilemmas

Dear Joseph,

The other night at dinner the phone rang, and for the umpteenth time this year it was some woman telemarketer trying to convince me to allow myself to be sent some credit card. I told her that I hoped she'd find some decent work instead of spending her time disrupting other people's family dinners. For good measure, I asked her for her home phone number so that I could return her call later, like at 2:00 A.M. When I hung up, my wife told me I sounded deranged, and was making a bad impression on the children. But I've had it up to here with these annoying calls. Tell me I'm right.

Disgusted

Dear Disgusted,

Had I received your letter just one week ago, I probably would have answered, "Right on!" and gone on to share with you other snappy retorts I have wanted to direct at these telemarketers.

But then, just a few days ago, I was speaking to my friend Charles Mizrahi, who told me that after years of reacting with great annoyance to such callers, he had undergone a change of heart. He'd asked himself one day, "Who are the people who are making these calls?" and concluded that most of them are probably either single mothers badly in need of money or people who take on a second job to bring in urgently needed cash.

By visualizing the financially strapped people making such calls, he felt more compassionate toward them. So the next time a call came, inevitably during dinnertime, he told the woman on the other end, "I don't think I'm interested in what you're selling, but I wish you success. Now I hope you'll excuse me, but I'm eating my dinner." The telemarketer was taken aback, and confided that in the week she had been doing this work, Charles was the first person who'd responded to her in a courteous manner. For this, she expressed much gratitude, even though she didn't make a sale.

"I know these calls are annoying," Charles said to me, "but the people making them are probably not in good circumstances, so there's no reason to be mean to them. Just act with compassion."

I was moved by what he said, but not fully convinced. After all, I reasoned, if we follow his example, maybe it will spur further growth in what I definitely hope is not a growth industry.

About an hour later, my phone rang. When I picked it up, I heard the inevitable question, "Is this Joseph Telushkin?" Only, of course, my name was drawn out and mispronounced, the immediate giveaway as to who was on the other end.

This time, however, I decided to use Charles's strategy. I listened for a few seconds, and then broke in. "You really don't have to give me your whole presentation," I said. "I'm not interested in buying your product. But I do hope you have greater success with others."

The woman thanked me, and I hung up.

And you know what I noticed? Not only was my being polite obviously pleasanter for the person making the call, but I myself felt better. Almost invariably, when I had received such calls in the past, I would announce, "I'm not interested," and more or less slam down the phone. But instead of feeling satisfied with myself, I would then be irritated, complaining to whoever was with me about how obnoxious these calls were. This time, after I hung up the phone, I felt no such annoyance. Instead, I felt good because I had been kind; I also felt a measure of compassion for the person who has to inflict herself on others by making these calls.

As is often the case, doing the right thing for another turned out to be the right thing for me, too.

Thank you, Charles.

Dear Joseph,

At a party a few months ago, when I was barely beginning to come to terms with the reality that my two-month-old baby was born with a severe disability, I mentioned my situation to another guest at the party. She replied, "You must be a very nice person—I don't believe that God would give such a baby to someone who wasn't good enough to take care of him." I was stunned, hurt, appalled, and angry. I thought, "No, God doesn't work that way—He wouldn't do that to me." I wanted to put her in her place but was too taken aback and, despite my fury, worried that I'd show my bile to someone who was probably well intentioned. What should I have said to her?

Hurt

Dear Hurt,

Did this woman have good intentions? Undoubtedly so. What she unfortunately lacked was common sense—both about God and about another's feelings. Analyze exactly what it was that she was saying. First, that she knows God's will. But how does she know why God sent you a baby with a disability? A medieval Hebrew proverb teaches, "If I knew God, I'd be God." This woman doesn't know God and isn't God. And thank God for that. For if she were God, she would discourage people from being good by making it known that the better they were, the more likely that God would reward them by sending them babies with disabilities.

Like many well-meaning but verbally impulsive or foolish people, she probably spoke without thinking. If you could explain to her why her comment was wounding, she might realize her error, apologize, and, most important, not continue hurting people with comments like this in the future. Therefore, perhaps you could have said to her something like "I know you meant well, but you should know that your words hurt me. For one thing, the implication of your comment—'if only I were a less nice person, I would have had a normal baby'—is a very painful thought. Furthermore, how would you feel if someone said to you, 'You seem like such a nice person that I pray God will reward you by causing you to have many babies with special needs'?"

Dear Joseph,

Is it immoral for a person to be overweight, particularly in the context of marriage? Do I "owe" it to my partner to be thin? My greatest fault is that, though I have many other good qualities, I am overweight. I'm successful in my work; my young adult children are productive members of society; I have friends and get along with everyone in my family. There is little in my life that is out of control, but this one thing. My husband feels that my being overweight is a direct reflection on him—that it says to other people that he's somehow defective because he chose to marry a thin person who became overweight. I'm tired of not being able to have a close, comfortable relationship with him because I never know when he is going to say something that will crush me again. I accept full responsibility for my being overweight— I blame it on no one but myself. But I really just want to be accepted for who I am, not what I look like.

Overweight and Insulted

Dear Overweight and Insulted,

Before I try to respond to your letter, I would like to remove the word *immoral* from this discussion. It's not helpful, because it's the kind of term that can be applied to, and demoralize, almost every individual for some personal failing. Are smokers immoral? Are diabetics who break their diet and eat food with sugar immoral? I believe that people who drink a lot of liquor when they know they will be driving a car later are acting immorally, but giving in to the normal range of human frailties—when they don't directly harm another—should not fall into the category of being immoral. In this context, it's too emotionally charged, inappropriate, and counterproductive a word.

Having said that, I find your letter one of the hardest to answer of any I've received. For one thing, I still don't have enough information. For example, when you say, "I accept full responsibility for my being overweight," what do you mean? The truth is, a lot of people can't control their weight or at least can't do so without extraordinary effort. The almost casual way in which you write that you accept full responsibility makes it sound as if you believe you could control your weight. If that is the case, then why don't you? For if you can control your weight without extraordinary effort, I do understand your husband's annoyance, though nothing justifies his making comments that "crush" you. You say that "I really just want to be accepted for who I am," and yet, when you met your husband, you were thin, so perhaps he had the right to expect that that's a part of who you are.

For better or for worse, women tend to be more tolerant than men of physical imperfection in the opposite sex. As a woman I know said to me when I read her your letter, "It's impossible for me to imagine a woman leaving a man she loved because he became overweight." Men are more apt to be drawn to a woman just because she is physically attractive. Unfortunately, if a woman's physical appeal played a large role in a man's initial attraction to her, it makes sense that a significant decrease in her attractiveness might well lead to a decrease in the man's interest in her.

Equally important, you use the word *overweight* without defining its degree. *Overweight* can mean anything from 15 pounds to 150 and more. The degree is important—I can imagine readers who would be horrified by your husband's great annoyance if you are 20 or 30 pounds overweight being more understanding of his reaction if you are a hundred pounds overweight. But again, nothing justifies his cruel comments.

In truth, many people can't control their weight very much. A friend told me how his wife gave birth to their four children during the first five years of their marriage, and put on much weight during the pregnancies. She has had great difficulty removing this weight. He loves her deeply, and appreciates that she put on the weight while pregnant with their children. He also appreciates the fact that she works hard at her diet, and although she hasn't yet been able to eliminate the excess weight, she hasn't given up. As she said to him, if she gives up on trying to diet, who knows how much more weight she might put on? My friend is deeply moved by his wife's efforts. It sounds to me, and I might be wrong, that you have sort of given up on trying to work on your weight. If that is the case, the fact that you're not trying to lose weight might be the trigger for much of your husband's anger. You sound like an exemplary human being, successful in your work, with fine children and many friends. It could be hurtful to your husband that you convey the impression that you make efforts for everybody else, but are not making an effort to be attractive to him. From his perspective, he may feel he's being taken for granted, a feeling that can trigger both hurt and anger.

Because of the hostility this issue seems to be generating, it probably would be wise for the two of you to see a marriage counselor. That you feel you can no longer have a close and comfortable relationship with your husband is very sad. And the insights of a good therapist might help you both find a better way to deal with your weight. You might be motivated to do more about it, and he might be motivated to be kinder to the person to whom he most owes kindness, his spouse.

Postscript: Rarely have I found my self-image as a pretty kind and sensitive person so under assault as I did after posting this column. Nothing I've ever written has triggered so many hostile responses. As one writer, who was politer than most, put it, "Losing weight is not an obligation to others, and to think so is very selfish. I'm surprised that your answer was so shallow. . . . There's obviously a much deeper issue going on here that you didn't even address."

Since I mentioned and criticized the husband's cruel comments to his wife several times, I wonder what the deeper issue was that my critic was thinking of. I suspect that the issue of being overweight is so sensitive that few of my correspondents noticed my repeated criticism of the husband. Instead, they saw me as supporting his behavior. A woman named Elizabeth wrote, "She is being abused by her husband, and you are suggesting that her physical appearance is eliciting this abuse. No one has the right to abuse another. . . . You just blamed the victim and killed the messenger."

Two other readers drew angry parallels between a woman's being overweight and male baldness (they picked the right man at whom to direct their comments; little hair adorns my head). As one put it, "I hope Telushkin doesn't mind if I alter the subhead of his article: 'Going Bald Isn't a Crime, but It Can Send a Message to Those You Love.' Right, Joe? The message it sends is that balding guys have sort of given up on trying to work on their hairlines. That they are not making an effort to be attractive to their wives. . . . So, Joe, for a male who is so eager to blame a woman for not looking 'attractive enough,' you don't mind if women hold males responsible for not looking attractive enough, do you?"

Occasionally, I wonder if some of my correspondents are actually responding to something that I wrote or to painful associations triggered by the subject of my column.

So let me offer three final thoughts, in as clear, and I hope as nonobnoxious, a manner as I can:

1. Cruel comments are abusive, and are always wrong.

2. One of life's unfair aspects is that most women tend to be more tolerant of physical imperfections in men, including baldness, than men are of physical imperfections in women.

3. Finally, and perhaps most significant, I may have been naive in taking literally the questioner's comment "I accept full responsibility for my being overweight—I blame it on no one but myself." If I erred in taking the woman at her word, with its implication that she could remove at least some of

her excess weight, then I, like her, take responsibility as well.

Dear Joseph,

In responding to a woman whose husband was mean to her because she was overweight, you wrote that "one of life's unfair aspects is that women tend to be more tolerant of physical imperfections in men than men are of physical imperfections in women." It seems to me that there is a big implication to what you are saying, that women—by not judging men by their looks the way men judge women—are deeper and morally superior to men. I don't have the sense that you're a big feminist, so what do you say to that?

Women Are Kinder

Dear Women Are Kinder,

If this were the only issue distinguishing men from women, then you'd be right: Greater openness to men who are not physically attractive would show women to be emotionally and morally deeper than men.

The problem is that while women are more tolerant than men in the area of looks, women, like men, tend to have their own areas of shallowness—specifically, money and professional success. Thus, if you were trying to fix up a man with a woman and told him, "She's gorgeous, bright, and very kind, but she's not that motivated professionally. I don't think she'll ever be a big earner," most men I know would think, "If she's gorgeous, bright, and very kind, I really want to meet her. I can make peace with the fact that she won't bring home a fat paycheck."

On the other hand, if you told most (though obviously not all) women, "There's a guy to whom I want to introduce you. He's really good-looking, bright, and kind, but not all that successful professionally," I suspect that a far higher percentage of middle-class (the group of people whom I know best) women would think, "Well, he sounds very nice, but this lack of ambition and low earning abilities sounds worrisome. I think I'll pass on this one."

A number of women to whom I've outlined this scenario acknowledge that what I've written is true, but say that such reasoning does not reflect badly on their sex. One woman noted that a lack of professional success in a man is itself a turnoff, while another said, "When a woman looks at a man, she's thinking of building a family with him, and she wants to know that he'll be motivated to support her and their children. There's nothing shallow about that. Security is a more serious consideration than looks."

Perhaps, but I'm only saying that your argument doesn't convince me that women are morally superior to men. In fact, I've long suspected that for many women, money plays the role that looks play for most men, enough certainly to earn one a first date, and maybe more. That's why when we hear of an older man married to a much younger woman, we generally assume that he's rich and she's pretty. When was the last time you saw a thirty-year-old woman on the arm of a man living off his social-security check? Or, as I recently heard a female comic say, "Viagra has existed among women for thousands of years. It's called money." (On the other hand, whether it's fair or unfair, when people hear of a young man with a much older woman, they often assume he has a need for a mother figure.)

In truth, it's a bad idea to turn this into a "Who's better?" issue, because life is more complex than that. The attraction of many women to wealth (and there are no shortage of men who are attracted to wealth as well) is motivated, in part, by a desire to have a safe environment for their future family, and by their attraction to the ambition and vitality of a man who's made himself rich (obviously, this would not follow if the man's wealth was inherited). Also, a woman might well feel nurtured by such a man, and as a woman who is very dear to me reminds me, "The combinations of affection and nurturing are an aphrodisiac to a woman."

And what about the tremendous emphasis that many men put on women's looks? I see it as largely, though not exclusively, due to males possessing a sexual organ that responds involuntarily. In contrast, many women find that as they become increasingly friendly with a man to whom they were not initially attracted, the man often becomes more physically attractive to them.

If the average man, on the other hand, is not physically attracted to a woman when they first meet, he will not feel physically attracted to her, even if they become friends, and even if she is the kindest and most nurturing of people. It is because the male sex organ has a mind of its own and responds involuntarily that looks have come to play so important— I'll acknowledge, too important—a role in how men determine which women to date and marry. (I've even heard men try to articulate a moral rationale to justify their pursuit only of women they find beautiful: "If I marry a woman who has a great character, but to whom I'm not very attracted, I'll probably find myself lusting after other women, and end up committing adultery.")

There are some fortunate mitigating factors. Most important, tastes in attractiveness are in no way uniform. I've noticed plenty of married women who don't meet Western standards of beauty. Similarly, I have heard men wax poetic about their wives' appearance, even though few other males would share their assessment. "Beauty," as has been drummed into our heads since childhood, "is in the eye of the beholder."

The greater truth is that, as a rule, physical attractiveness will more easily help a woman secure more male interest, while a man's professional success is more likely to interest many women.

Is this fair? No.

Does this reflect badly on both sexes? Yes.

So what else is new?

Dear Joseph,

   I know smoking is bad, but am I a bad person if I smoke? A lot of people seem to think so. It's legal to smoke in restaurants in my state, but when I light up, you should see the looks I get. People pointedly ask me to move to another table, or actually turn around and scold me. Even my friends think it's a moral failing. What's your opinion?

Guilty Smoker

Dear Guilty Smoker,

   Smoking is a self-destructive habit. There's a good chance it will take years off your life, and thereby cause you and people dear to you great pain. Having said that, I find the demonization of smokers so common today to be excessive and, on occasion, cruel. A few years ago, the California Department of Health Services produced a television ad asserting that secondhand smoke may cause sudden infant death syndrome (SIDS). The SIDS Alliance sent a letter to the Department of Health Services protesting the ad, since there's *no* compelling evidence to document this assertion. The cruelty of such an ad was underscored in an essay by Dennis Prager, "The War Against Tobacco and America's Broken Moral Compass": "For any parent[s] who smoked and lost a child to SIDS, a largely inexplicable child killer, this ad, charging them with the killing of their child, can only be described as devastating. . . . One can only imagine the effect on couples who lost a child to SIDS and who believe this television ad—the guilt felt by the smoking parent for killing his or her baby, and the anger felt by the non-smoking parent at the other parent."

While smoking is self-destructive, there's ample reason to believe that the damage caused by secondhand smoke has been exaggerated. (If research reveals secondhand smoke to be very damaging, then I will have to revise my views on the immorality of smoking.) Therefore, smoking doesn't make you a bad person any more than eating too many sweets or not exercising makes you a bad person, though either behavior might shorten your life. What's next? Are we going to start calling people who sleep too few hours at night evil? Perhaps we should, since a lack of sufficient sleep definitely increases the likelihood of getting into a car accident in which others might be injured or killed. What about people who drink alcohol? Are they bad people, given that a small but significant percentage of people who consume liquor wind up doing very evil things, such as rape, murder, and child and spousal abuse (which, by the way, is not the case with smoking).

On the other hand, because smoking is so likely to harm smokers, I would regard a person who participated in an ad campaign to convince nonsmokers, particularly minors, to start smoking to be doing something evil. And I would similarly regard as evil tobacco companies and executives who added elements to cigarettes to make them more addictive (particularly if they did so after they were already aware of smoking's baneful effects).

I also think it wise for parents to draw up contracts with their children to pay them a certain amount of money—and it should not be a trivial sum—if they reach the age of twenty-one without taking up this habit: Research shows that people who don't become addicted to cigarettes by twenty-one are unlikely ever to do so. Still, I oppose efforts to demonize smokers as people without moral character or backbone. It's now become common in many schools to tell young children that nicotine is an addictive drug, just like other, illegal, drugs. I suspect this has the effect not of making nicotine seem horrific but of making drugs like heroin seem not so bad; after all, many children see their parents smoke without otherwise acting irresponsibly or out of control. Children whose parents indulge in heroin and other illegal drugs have far worse memories of their childhood than do children whose parents smoke cigarettes.

If people complain about your smoking in a restaurant that has set aside a smokers' section, it's their responsibility to move, not yours. Obviously, if somebody is bothered by your smoking in a home you are visiting, or if somebody is visiting your home and complains about the smoke, common courtesy dictates that you cease smoking. Also, because many people bothered by smoke might be hesitant to complain, particularly when they are in your house, I believe you should ask visitors if it will bother them if you smoke.

At a time when the antismoking campaign has

become so widespread, the point that must be emphasized over and over again is that smoking overwhelmingly is a health issue, not a moral one. I would therefore suggest that you try whatever technique it takes to rid yourself of this habit, except one: thinking of yourself as a bad person because you smoke.

✺

Dear Joseph,

Lately, several of the highest-profile people in my industry, who are known for their cruelty to employees (including me) as well as for their talent, have been failing miserably and publicly. Their staffs are deserting them in droves. I'm trying not to gloat, but I am. Can you help me?

Gloating

Dear Gloating,

Your question implies that you're feeling guilty. Yet, if your letter is an accurate portrayal of what's happened, perhaps you shouldn't. What exactly is wrong about feeling happy that people known for their "cruelty to employees" are experiencing professional failure? The alternative—being happy at their successes—would also mean feeling happy at their opportunity to go on being cruel to others who are unfortunate enough to work for them.

Does this mean that all gloating about the sufferings of those who have hurt us is okay? No. What exonerates you in this case is that you're experiencing happiness that these people's cruelty in the workplace is now being rewarded by the workplace's being cruel to them. However, it would be wrong, and destructive of your character, to gloat if they were forced to resign their positions because, say, they needed to take care of a child stricken with a virulent disease. Or, for that matter, if they themselves were so stricken. In such a case, you might be pleased that they no longer were in a position to hurt others, but it would be wrong to rejoice in their personal anguish.

When we dislike someone who's experiencing suffering, we may be tempted to say, "Serves them right." But I would hold my tongue. For undoubtedly there are people whom I've hurt, and who believe some pretty awful fates would serve me right.

The question is, how much gloating is okay? It seems to me that it's all right to express your pleasure to friends and relatives, and to present or former fellow suffering employees, all of whom are aware of how much you suffered while working for the "highest-profile people" who are now getting their comeuppance. But limit the number of people to whom you speak about the situation, and don't go out of your way to describe your experiences and your gloating to those who aren't already in the know. This is self-serving advice as well. Rejoicing at the suffering of others won't do much for your reputation; people may well conclude that you're a vindictive person. Also, now that these people have fallen, see if you can distance yourself from your anger and find room in your heart for some compassion. I stress both words, *compassion* as well as *some*.

Finally, if you want some good to come out of your gloating, think through what it is that these people did that really hurt you and others—and then make sure that you don't act similarly to other people. Many of us are geniuses at recalling every slight we've experienced, but have difficulty acknowledging the emotional suffering we inflict on others.

Dear Joseph,

The recent collapse in the stock market has not only devastated me financially, I think it's starting to have an ugly impact on my character. I find I spend a lot of time talking to friends about what's happened to our lives financially, and whenever I hear of people who've suffered losses as bad as mine or even worse, I feel better, even happy. I mean, the fact that these people are losing money doesn't get me back any of my own, so there's no reason for me to feel pleased about this. But I do. Are my own losses turning me into a bad person?

Mean-Spirited Loser

Dear Mean-Spirited Loser,

If this quirk of yours—feeling somewhat better when you hear of other people's financial losses—is the sole evidence of your character deterioration, I wouldn't be too worried. If, God forbid, you had been diagnosed with a life-threatening illness, and found yourself happy to hear of others also contracting this illness, I would argue that that would be indicative of a real fault in character. In general, the fact that you are miserable is no reason to derive satisfaction from others also being miserable.

But in the case of the stock market, I don't think it's rottenness of character that is responsible for your deriving satisfaction from hearing about the losses of others. Rather, when people lose money in a bad investment, they don't just feel impoverished, they also feel stupid. And the belief that they have acted stupidly makes them feel humiliated: "How could I have been so dumb as to not realize how overpriced the market was, that it was a bubble, that it had to collapse?" Therefore, I suspect that the gratification you feel when you learn about others, people whom you view as being as intelligent as you are and who have suffered as you have, has less to do with the fact that they are suffering than with the fact that you no longer feel singled out for being a fool: "Look how bright some of these people are. If they were as misguided as I was, that must mean that I simply made an understandable mistake."

Of course, the fact that you derive pleasure from hearing of others who've made the same mistakes as you have is not a noble character trait, and I suspect you may not qualify for sainthood (saints, I imagine, are not the sort of people who play the market), but it is an understandable reaction to the painful experience of losing much of your nest egg. As long as you don't carry this emotion to an extreme (such as being happy when you hear of a family that has to move because they can't make their mortgage payments), I don't think you need to castigate yourself. However, if you are the sort of person who prays to God to help you in your daily life, why don't you try for the next few weeks to first offer prayers on behalf of some of your friends who are suffering in the way you are. As you do, you will find yourself empathizing with their pain, frustration, and fear, and that will definitely be good for your character.

Dear Joseph,

I have done a lot of sins in my life. I am eleven years old, and my birthday is coming up soon. What should I do to make those sins go away?

Sinner

Dear Sinner,

It is a little hard for me to answer your important question because you don't tell me what sort of sins you've committed. If you've done things that have hurt other people, is there a way you can undo the damage? Also, can you go to these people and ask them if they would forgive you for what you did? Most people, when approached, will act in a forgiving way.

Have you perhaps committed acts that go against your religious tradition, and are therefore sins against God? I once read of a wise rabbi who asked his followers, "How do we know when God has forgiven a sin we have committed?" Nobody answered, so the rabbi said, "We know by the fact that we no longer commit that sin."

Have you really done "a lot of sins," as you write? Perhaps you have, but maybe you're judging yourself too harshly, which is often the sign of a truly good person (who holds him- or herself to a higher standard). If you're a member of a church or synagogue, may I suggest that you speak to a minister, priest, or rabbi to whom you might be able to confide the acts that are causing you to feel guilt, and ask him or her to suggest what you might do to repent and relieve yourself of these unhappy feelings?

One final thought: You can't make the sins go away. But if you become a somewhat different person, those sins will become quite irrelevant, as if they were committed by a different person, the old you.

☙

Dear Joseph,

I am having difficulty relating to friends and neighbors who are living together outside of marriage. Please advise.

Unhappily Judgmental

Dear Unhappily Judgmental,

Two very dear friends of mine have lived together for over a decade. They have two children, but no marriage license; the woman, a dyed-in-the-wool, 1960s-style feminist, believes that the institution of marriage has been used throughout history to oppress women. They are among the most devoted couples and parents I know.

Do I wish they would get married? Yes, but it's not something I think about much, even though I see them often. So now I have a question for you: What is it that most bothers you about people who live together—that they aren't married or that they seem uncommitted to each other? Or, if they have children, that they seem uncommitted to their children? If it's the latter, I agree with you; you're right to have trouble relating to them (you'd also be right in having trouble relating to a married couple who were not committed to their children).

However, if your discomfort is primarily a response to people's living together without being married, I would simply say that, as a rule, I believe it is much better for people to marry, and it is most certainly almost always better for children to come into the world with married parents. Having said that, I also believe that it's much better for one's own equanimity and happiness to not be too bothered by other people's living arrangements.

Dear Joseph,

I have an ethical quandary in the realm of hurt feelings. My fiancée and I were due to be married this summer by our temple's rabbi, who had agreed last autumn to perform the service. Early this spring, he announced that he was taking a yearlong sabbatical from the synagogue and called our parents to apologize that he would not be able to officiate. Although we have since found a rabbi, and the wedding will proceed, I find myself beset by "hard" feelings toward our previous rabbi. What upsets me is that he never called us personally to apologize, although he had spoken with us personally when he agreed to perform the ceremony. I'm also finding myself less receptive to what he says in his sermons and writings because of these hard feelings. How can I get over this?

Angry and Hurt

Dear Angry and Hurt,

Boy, is my face red. I thank you for your sensitivity in writing in the third person about the rabbi who disappointed you, but I realized by the end of the first few sentences that I was the culprit. For this I humbly apologize. Your letter made me realize my insensitivity in not contacting you directly. Indeed, your words contain two important moral lessons—one obvious, and one more subtle.

First, in a situation in which someone will be disappointed, the "disappointer" must think very carefully about which people will be affected by his or her behavior and make sure to be in contact with each one of them directly. To do so isn't just an issue of politeness, but also a moral issue, because people's feelings are involved. In my lectures, I often speak of exercising "moral imagination," which means that one should use the full range of one's intellect to avoid inflicting not only obvious hurts, but also more subtle ones. In your case, the person who originally called to ask me to perform the wedding was your mother, and hers was the only phone number in my diary. So when I realized that I would not be able to perform the wedding, she was the person I called.

I should have realized that this one call would not be sufficient, since it is your wedding, and the event is understandably very important to you. In most cases, hurt feelings can be avoided or minimized by being in touch directly with the affected party.

The less obvious moral lesson in your letter was that you wrote it at all. When one has a grievance against someone, it's best to tell him or her directly rather than simply complain about the matter to others. Most people do just the opposite—they don't contact the person who's angered them, but instead share their annoyance with others, thereby injuring the reputation of the person who offended them and never coming to a satisfying closure.

I am therefore grateful that you contacted me directly. It reminded me of an incident that happened several years ago. A reader took strong exception to something I had written about a specific Jewish teaching. He managed to obtain my phone number, called me, and very respectfully but firmly asked me to explain why I had taken the position I did. After I had explained myself, it was clear that he still disagreed with me. But at least he realized that I hadn't taken my position out of malicious intent. Had he instead condemned my teachings to others, not only would he have damaged my name, but he also probably would have ended up feeling much worse about me, attributing to me bad motives, as well as an incorrect position.

I hope you realize that my apology is heartfelt, and that you will forgive me. I am reminded of William Blake's old quatrain:

> *I was angry with my friend:*
> *I told my wrath, my wrath did end.*
> *I was angry with my foe:*
> *I told it not, my wrath did grow.*

And finally, I wish you a happy marriage, one in which your honesty and openness with your spouse will lead to a lifetime of happiness and mutual understanding.

Dear Joseph,

I live in a small building with no doorman in New York City. Four or five of us get the *New York Times* delivered every day; the papers are left near the front door. On a recent morning, when I went downstairs to pick up my paper, I noted that mine was missing. I hesitated, then took a neighbor's paper. But not just any neighbor's. I took the paper that belonged to a guy who had in fact cheated our co-op and, at least once, beaten his first wife (a bunch of us heard it). About a year ago, he illegally sublet his apartment, and, when he informed his tenant that she'd have to move out, he threatened to sic two thugs on her if she didn't do so promptly.

Just what combination of avenger, vigilante, thief, and/or minor offender do you think I am?

Paper Snatcher

P.S. Laws being what they are, we haven't been able to evict him.

Dear Paper Snatcher,

Your neighbor sounds like a disgusting person. Do you therefore have the right to steal his newspaper?

When phrased like that, the answer becomes pretty obvious. Of course not. And you, of course, know that.

The truth is, if your description of your neighbor is accurate, he deserves far worse than having his paper stolen. But still, taking his newspaper is not good for your soul.

You're rationalizing, and once you start rationalizing stealing, where will it end? "This hotel overcharges me, so it's okay if I take a few towels."

If we decide that whether or not we are permitted to steal from another depends on the would-be victim's character, things could deteriorate quickly: "That guy over there whose wallet fell is a disgusting person. Joanne told me he cheated her at his store. Maybe I'll keep the cash in his wallet and will even give Joanne ten dollars."

Having said that, there is one instance in which I can envision taking the man's paper: if you knew for a fact that he had stolen your paper. However, among your neighbor's manifold faults, stealing newspapers does not seem to be one.

Otherwise, I think you should suffer the discomfort, and go out and buy a paper. You'll feel better about yourself—and you'll avoid starting down a slippery slope that could take you to places you surely don't want to go.

Dear Joseph,

Most New Year's resolutions seem to revolve around losing weight, exercising, and giving up smoking. Do you have any ethical New Year's resolutions?

Looking to Make Myself Better

Dear Looking to Make Myself Better,

I have many ideas, but since one of them is not to bore people, and another is not to sound self-righteous, I'll restrict myself to two. But first, I want to say that starting the New Year with ethical resolutions is a wonderful idea. Two hundred years ago, the Hasidic rebbe Nachman of Bratslav offered this challenge to his followers: "If you are not going to be better tomorrow than you were today, then what need do you have for tomorrow?"

Reb Nachman's point is profound. If you don't grow in some manner each day, then your soul atrophies. How meaningful can your life be if your goodness is not expanding, if indeed you are no better tomorrow—or next year—than you were today?

With that in mind, let me suggest two activities that will improve the quality of your own life, and of those around you.

1. *Declare Periodic Complaining Fasts*

A complaining fast is like a food fast. In the same way that you refrain from eating for a full twenty-four hours during a fast, so you refrain from complaining about anything for a full day during a complaining fast (obviously, if something truly bad is going on, you can call attention to it). Such fasts might be invoked whenever the level of complaining in your house or office becomes excessive and demoralizing, which for most families probably happens once every two or three weeks.

In our family, what generally triggers such a fast is a scenario something like this: I come home in a happy mood, having had a good day at work. My wife, however, has had a difficult day, and she starts to tell me about it. At first I am very sympathetic, but the longer she talks about how difficult her day has been, the more I start to rethink mine: "You think you had a hard day; you know what happened to me?" Inside of ten minutes, we're both convinced that we're leading miserably unhappy lives. In response, we declare a complaining fast. Once complaining ceases to be an option, you quickly become more appreciative both of the people around you and of the good things going on in your life. A man told me that one night, just before he fell asleep, he reviewed his interactions with his ten-year-old daughter since he had come home from work, and realized that almost every one had been negative. He had walked into her room and reprimanded her for how sloppy it was; then, at the dinner table, he had become upset with her bad table manners. Later, he expressed annoyance that she hadn't yet done her homework, and when she did do it, he was upset at the mistakes she had made. He also knew that if, after this barrage of criticism, his daughter had said to him, "Daddy, do you really love me?" he would have answered, "Of course I do. The only reason I point out all these things is that I love you and want you to do better." But then he wondered how he would feel at work if his boss criticized him in such a relentless manner. Would he believe that the boss really cared about him, or would he conclude that the boss probably held him in contempt—and end up spending much of his work time feeling demoralized?

Complaining fasts liberate us to notice and comment upon the good things in the people around us. You'll feel better about your life, and I assure you that the people who interact with you will feel better about you and about themselves.

2. *Say a Prayer When You Hear an Ambulance Go By*

As I first noted in *The Book of Jewish Values*, I often used to feel annoyed when a conversation in which I was engaged was shattered by the loud siren of a passing ambulance. Several years ago, when I confided my embarrassment about this reaction to my friend Rabbi Zalman Schachter Shalomi, he offered this advice: "Whenever you hear an ambulance, offer a prayer that the ambulance arrives in time. Make a similar prayer when you hear the blaring siren of a fire truck or police car."

When I started making such prayers, two things happened. I stopped feeling annoyed, because I had something constructive to do. And then, after a few days, I realized that through this prayer I had started practicing "Love your neighbor as yourself," even toward "neighbors" I had never met, and never would. Imagine if this prayer became widely practiced, and one day, God forbid, you were in an ambulance, and knew that wherever the ambulance passed, people were praying for you.

On that note, I conclude by wishing you a good today and an even better tomorrow.

Dear Joseph,

My neighbor is a born-again Christian who believes that people who don't accept Jesus will go to hell. Personally, I don't care what he believes; it's a free country. The problem is that he feels a moral need to save me from hell. I find that I now avoid going out for the mail if I see him standing outside. Any opportunity that presents itself, he tries to convince me that Jesus and God are one, and I must have faith in Jesus. My reaction? I want to tell *him* to go to hell. Should I?

Between Heaven and Hell

Dear Between Heaven and Hell,

Some years ago, I was on a radio panel consisting of a minister, a priest, and a rabbi (me). At one point, the moderator asked each of us to address a question to one of our fellow clergy. I asked the minister—like your neighbor, a born-again fundamentalist—the following: "As a religious Jew, I accept the Torah as the word of God, even though there are a few things in it that I wish weren't there. For example, I wish the Bible had outlawed slavery. Torah law made it more moderate and humane than slavery as practiced in the rest of the world, but I wish it had just outlawed it. I know that your understanding of the New Testament leads you to believe that people who don't have faith in Jesus will go to hell. I wonder if you at least wish that the New Testament didn't teach that, or if you're happy that there is such a teaching there."

As is often the case, I remember my question better than the response. But my experience with this minister, and yours with your neighbor, reminds me of the reason I find such a belief to be so unfortunate. To my mind, there's something very wrong in believing that what matters most to God is what a person believes, not what he or she does. Also, as a committed Jew, I know how the Christian preoccupation with faith influenced many people in the past to behave badly toward those who didn't share their faith. Many Crusaders, for example, used to offer medieval Jews the choice of accepting Jesus as their savior or being killed. Tens, and more likely hundreds, of thousands of Jews throughout history were murdered because they wouldn't accept the belief that God's first demand of human beings is faith in Jesus.

The good news today is that we live in a democracy, so while your neighbor can try to persuade you to share his beliefs, he cannot coerce you. And I suspect that he has no desire to do so. Christian fundamentalists today are, by and large, very different from fundamentalists in the past. Thus, some years ago, American Jews were outraged when a very prominent fundamentalist Baptist, the Reverend Bailey Smith, declared that "God doesn't hear the prayers of Jews [because all prayers must be directed to or via Jesus]." But in the very next sentence, Reverend Smith proclaimed that he would defend to the death the right of Jews to offer prayers as they wished. This is certainly not the sort of teaching that an antisemitic fundamentalist like Martin Luther would have offered.

Therefore, I would urge you not to regard your neighbor as an evil person. I believe he suffers from the ailment he attributes to you: bad beliefs. But he is not a bad person. He really does want to do you a favor, and save you from eternal damnation (though you and I might agree that a God who would damn people for not having certain right beliefs is unworthy of being God). I therefore think that you should resist the temptation to tell him to go to hell, and say to him as follows:

> Thank you for caring about me. But just as you have thought about your religious convictions and have come to certain conclusions, so have I. I think your conclusions are wrong, and you think mine are. You've already made your views known to me, and if I ever choose to reconsider, I'll discuss the matter with you. Till then, I'd prefer not to talk about it. If such an attitude condemns me to hell, so be it. It won't be your fault, because you've made an effort to expose me to your truth. If this means we cannot be friends, I accept that. But if you persist in trying to convert me, we certainly cannot be friends. I hope you'll decide that in fact we can be.

I hope a comment like this, or some version of it, will buy you some peace.

¥.

Dear Joseph,

As a single guy in his late twenties who's doing okay professionally, I get fixed up on a lot of dates.

Most turn out to be nonstarters, but at the evening's end, I almost always tell the woman, "I'll call you," even though in most cases I won't. I do it so that the evening won't have all these awkward silences at the end. Also, I do think it's a kind thing to say, a way of saying, "I enjoyed the time I spent with you." A friend of mine, a single guy, too, says he's honest; if he's not going to call, he won't lead the woman to think he will. He thinks I'm a liar; I think he's needlessly hurtful. What do you think?

White Liar

Dear White Liar,

I think your friend is right, and it's not because I'm addicted to always telling the truth. There are times, most notably when people's feelings are involved, that mistruths are appropriate, particularly when no good can be gained by telling the truth. For example, take a widow who tells you tearfully what a good man her recently deceased husband was—an opinion you don't happen to share. If she then says, "You liked him too, didn't you?" I would advise a tactful concurrence. Similarly, if a young child asks whether you like his drawing, which seems to you to bear no relationship to what the child tells you he was trying to draw, you should, nonetheless, tell the child how much you like it. In other words, white lies are untruths that are meant not to secure an advantage for yourself, but rather to spare another's feelings.

The white lies that you tell do not spare feelings, but may actually cause far more hurt. The woman whom you dated might have liked you, and when the phone rings she might be hoping it's you. When she eventually realizes that you were feeding her a line, she will probably feel both hurt and humiliated. I suspect that your lies are not intended to spare your date's feelings as much as they are intended to spare yourself awkwardness at the end of an evening. It is true that many women know this line might be a lie and will not be hurt by its use, but others will wait for a call that never comes. Why add unnecessary pain to a world that already has too much pain?

You do not need to be brutally honest; just avoid being hurtful. At the end of the evening, thank the woman for a nice time (even if it wasn't, this is an acceptable white lie), and tell her you're pleased that you met (ditto). A friend told me, "When I was single, I once told a date, with much trepidation, 'I think you're a lovely woman, but I just don't think we're that compatible.' To my pleasant surprise, rather than being angry, or hurt, she thanked me for my honesty, and told me how often men had deceived her about their true feelings."

And what should you do if the woman is forward and actually asks, "Would you like to get together again?" To that, I don't have a good answer, so I'm going to turn to my readers for some responses, and, God willing, we will publish the best ones in this book's paperback edition.

EIGHT

Community

Dear Joseph,

I'd like you to settle an argument that's been raging between two of my friends and me for over a week now. I say *Who Wants to Marry a Multimillionaire?* was about the most immoral thing I've ever seen on TV; it seemed like a form of legalized prostitution. My friends, whom I generally think of as pretty good people, argue that because no one was coerced to do anything against his or her will, the show wasn't immoral. So tell me, Mr. Ethics, who's right?

Perplexed and Angry

Dear Perplexed and Angry,

For that small percentage of Americans who might not recall the TV special *Who Wants to Marry a Multimillionaire?*, let me briefly explain the show's premise (since I didn't see it, I'm basing my summary on what I've read. I'm also pleased to note that the show ran only one time). An unmarried man who, it was claimed, had been examined and found to have assets in excess of $2 million remained hidden throughout almost the entire show and watched as fifty women (selected from some two thousand volunteers) paraded in bathing suits before him and the audience and answered a variety of questions. Each woman, hard as it is for me to believe, had agreed in advance that if the man selected her, she would immediately marry him on national television. At the program's end, the man did select one woman, and the couple wed publicly (very shortly thereafter the marriage ended; it was, I believe, annulled).

Although the show appealed to the lowest form of human greed, I don't ipso facto condemn it as immoral, for the same reason that your friends don't. The women who appeared on the program knew exactly why they were there (to marry a wealthy man), and the man knew exactly why they wanted to marry him (because he was rich). Such behavior is greedy, even disgusting, but it is not, in my view, immoral. Immoral would be, for example, if a woman told a wealthy man that she loved him and wanted to marry him, when she knew all along that what she most loved about him was his money and that absent his wealth, she would never consider marrying him. Equally immoral would be a man who proclaimed his love for a woman only to induce her to sleep with him.

You dismiss the show, in my view justifiably, as almost being "a form of legalized prostitution."

Does my reluctance therefore to declare the program immoral mean that I don't regard prostitution as immoral? In theory, I don't (in practice, prostitution is very often immoral because it involves pimps exploiting young women who often come from emotionally, physically, and sexually abusive homes, so the choices they make to become prostitutes are not fully free-will decisions).

I believe that prostitution is debasing to the human spirit and unholy, because it converts the act of loving into a business transaction. But, if a woman *freely* chooses (that is, she could earn money doing other types of work) to accept money from a man in exchange for sleeping with him, I don't see the act in and of itself as immoral. I realize that many people, particularly those on the religious right and many feminists on the left, would disagree with me. Regarding the feminists, I am somewhat puzzled by their opposition, since they are committed to the belief that a woman should have the right to do what she wants with her body. Does that mean that they believe a woman has the right to do what she wants with her body only when she wants to abort a fetus but not when she has made the decision to sell her body for sex? Again, I am not advocating prostitution; it is about as unholy an act as I can imagine. I am only arguing that if the relationship is entered into freely, it is not clear to me why this should be condemned as immoral.

Who Wants to Marry a Multimillionaire? reminded me of a famous story told of George Bernard Shaw, who once met a beautiful woman at a party and asked her if she would sleep with a man for a million pounds.

"I would," the woman answered.

"And would you sleep with a man for five pounds?"

The woman grew indignant. "What do you think I am?" she asked.

Shaw responded, "We've already established what you are. Now, we're just haggling over the price."

The moment a woman—or for that matter, a man—agrees to marry a person on the basis of that person's wealth, she has converted the bonds of marriage into a form of prostitution. But such is the case only if the woman makes it known to the man that money is the only reason she is marrying him; the man, therefore, is not being misled. However, if she tells him that she loves him when she doesn't, her act is morally worse than prostitution, since it involves a serious deception through an emotionally exploitative lie.

The Talmud, the two-thousand-year-old compilation and code of Jewish legal teachings, states, "Whoever marries a woman for her money"—the Talmud clearly recognizes that such marriages go in both directions—"will have disreputable children." The meaning is that the father will have children who will, on the basis of his example, do anything for money.

Unfortunately, such behavior is all too common.

Over the years, many people have told me that they were raised with parental maxims such as "You shouldn't marry for money, but then again it's just as easy to fall in love with a rich girl [or rich boy] as a poor one."

In truth, marrying for money often leads to misery not only for the well-off partner who married under the assumption that he or she was loved, but also for the unscrupulous spouse. As my friend the late Rabbi Wolfe Kelman used to say, "Whoever marries for money ends up paying for it."

In brief, then, is the premise of *Who Wants to Marry a Multimillionaire?* immoral? No. Just despicable.

Dear Joseph,

I have some religious friends who vehemently support capital punishment for murderers. This strikes me as ridiculous, since, as religious people, shouldn't they at least support the Ten Commandments, which legislate, "You shall not kill"?

Disappointed

Dear Disappointed,

Before you read the rest of this response, sit down for a moment, since the next sentence might shock you. The Ten Commandments does not state, "You shall not kill." The correct translation of the

Hebrew is "You shall not murder." Like English, Hebrew has separate words for *killing (harog)* and *murder (ratzoch)*.

Murder is always forbidden, because it involves killing an innocent person, one who does not deserve to die. Killing is wrong the overwhelming majority of the time, but not always. That is why we speak, for example, of "killing in self-defense," not "murdering" in self-defense.

Had the biblical law said, "You shall not kill," that would have constituted a categorical prohibition of killing, including killing in self-defense. Such a prohibition would mean that a nation attacked by another would be forbidden to defend itself, since doing so would inevitably result in the killing of enemy soldiers.

However, the strongest proof that the Bible did not intend to prohibit the death sentence is that the law mandating capital punishment for premeditated murderers is the *only* law that occurs in all five books of the Torah, the first and most authoritative section of the Hebrew Bible.

- Genesis 9:6 teaches, "Whoever sheds the blood of man, by man shall his blood be shed, for in His image did God make man." This law, which was mandated long before God's covenant with Abraham, prescribed the death sentence for those who intentionally shed innocent blood. It was intended for all of humankind, not just Israelites.

- Exodus 21:12 decrees, "He who fatally strikes a man shall be put to death." This law applies only to premeditated killers, as indicated by the following verse: "If he did not do it by design . . . I will assign you a place to which he [the killer] can flee."
- Leviticus 24:17 rules, "Whoever takes the life of any human being shall be put to death."
- Numbers 35:31 prohibits a practice common in the ancient world: a murderer freeing himself from punishment by paying a ransom to the victim's family. In opposing this practice, the Bible rules, "You shall not accept ransom for the life of a murderer who is guilty of a capital crime; he must be put to death."
- Deuteronomy 19:11–13 warns people not to regard a murderer with pity, but rather to execute him and purge the land "of the blood of the innocent."

The rationale for executing murderers seems to emanate from the Bible's belief that *innocent* life possesses *infinite* value. Therefore, one who murders an innocent person has committed an infinite evil, and a lesser punishment than death would not fit the crime. Because the Bible wanted to make sure that innocent people weren't executed, it insisted on the testimony of at least two witnesses to the crime (see Numbers 35:30 and Deuteronomy 17:6). Indeed, influenced by the fear of executing an innocent person, many rabbis of the Talmud tried to limit executions of murderers.

Thus, you certainly have the right to oppose and

argue against capital punishment. But you're committing an error if you base your opposition on the Bible and the Ten Commandments.

✳

Dear Joseph,

In response to a letter several months ago in which the writer spoke critically of religious people who favored capital punishment, you wrote that the Bible approved of capital punishment for those who commit premeditated murders. The whole tone of your response suggested that you clearly favored the Bible's position. I'm curious if the recent well-publicized instances in which DNA evidence has shown that people who were sentenced to die were in reality innocent have caused you to reconsider your support of capital punishment?

More Than Curious

Dear More Than Curious,

In recent years, as you note, several people convicted of murder prior to, and/or without the use of, DNA evidence have proved to be innocent. These cases have greatly affected me. I believe that now that we have such a powerful tool as DNA, such evidence must be considered in all capital cases (cases of rape as well; in fact, all cases where someone might be sentenced to prison). Although it might be expensive, the cost is well worth it. For what could be more unjust than having an innocent person executed or, for that matter, incarcerated for life, when we have a technique that could have exonerated him or her?

The person most associated with the use of DNA to absolve convicted murderers and rapists is Barry Scheck, creator of the Innocence Project at Yeshiva University's Cardozo School of Law. Mr. Scheck has worked with remarkable diligence and is responsible for the release of a number of people who were wrongfully convicted.

However, Mr. Scheck also worked on the defense team at O. J. Simpson's trial. If the point of Scheck's involvement was to show that DNA evidence exonerated O. J., then part of me is suspicious about how such evidence can be used and possibly manipulated. For despite the jury's verdict in that case, I, like most Americans, believe that O. J. Simpson was guilty. I also believe that Mr. Scheck, if he indeed wants many Americans to take his Innocence Project seriously, should make a clear-cut statement, which until now he has not done, concerning the DNA evidence in the O. J. Simpson case. No damage could befall Mr. Simpson from Mr. Scheck's comments, since, even if he were to say he thought him guilty, O. J. could not be retried. In the absence of any statement by Mr. Scheck, some people will remain doubtful about the significance of other cases involving DNA in which Scheck has become involved. I write this with great respect for Mr. Scheck. Having spent an evening in dialogue with him, I found him to be a highly idealistic and impressive human being.

What people sometimes neglect to point out is that DNA evidence cuts both ways. Just as the lack of such evidence can point to a convicted defendant's innocence, its presence might point to a defendant's guilt. Thus, I continue to believe that in some instances capital punishment is appropriate. In addition to well-known cases such as that of Charles Manson (in which case DNA evidence would have been irrelevant since he ordered the murders of his victims but did not personally carry them out) and Sirhan Sirhan, consider the recent killings in New York City, in which two gunmen stole $2,000 from a Wendy's restaurant and murdered five employees because the criminals feared that these people might later testify against them. I believe that by their actions, these two murderers forfeited their own right to live.

However, I believe equally strongly that before we execute a murderer, we should have a standard of evidence that goes beyond a reasonable doubt.

⚸

Dear Joseph,

In a recent column, you wrote that if you lived in a society in which people were put to death for crimes such as robbery [see pages 76–77], and you had witnessed such a crime, you hoped you'd have the moral strength to offer false testimony and save the thief from death. By your logic, shouldn't a witness in a capital case who thinks the death penalty is barbaric be morally entitled to offer false testimony?

Against All Lying

Dear Against All Lying,

I would draw the following distinction: Two centuries ago in England, pickpockets could be hanged. Hanging someone for sticking his hand into another's pocket and extracting something (admittedly a wrongful act) is so disproportionate to the crime committed that I would argue that it is analogous to hanging an innocent person. Therefore, testifying that you saw someone pickpocketing would, in effect, bring about the killing of an innocent person. That is why I would justify lying in such a case (and it is not a justification I come to easily; perjury is a hideous crime that can undermine our entire judicial system. I would argue, however, that a system that hangs pickpockets deserves to be somewhat undermined).

But even if one regards capital punishment for acts of premeditated murder as barbaric, a witness who saw the deed or has important circumstantial evidence can hardly regard the person on trial as in any way innocent, or in danger of receiving a punishment disproportionate to the act he committed (the killer will have the same thing done to him as he did to another, just as I would favor a pickpocket being deprived of the money he stole from another). That is why lying in such a case would be wrong, even if one opposes capital punishment.

Dear Joseph,

In the aftermath of the attacks on the World Trade Center and the Pentagon (9/11/2001), it became immediately apparent that there are many people around the world who hate the United States. An enormous banner, photographed at a demonstration in Pakistan and shown in the *New York Times*, read, "Americans, think. Why are you hated all over the world?"

Shouldn't the widespread nature of such hatred prompt us to do some real soul-searching as to the evils we have done that could cause such animosity?

Feeling Guilty

Dear Feeling Guilty,

Consider the following Confucian dialogue:

Tse Kung asked Confucius, "What would you say if all the people in a village like a person?"

"That is not enough," replied Confucius.

"What would you say if all the people in a village dislike a person?"

"That is not enough," said Confucius. "It is better that the good people of the village like him, and the bad people of the village dislike him. When you are disliked by the bad person, you are a good person" (Lin Yutang, *The Wisdom of Confucius*).

That the United States today is hated by people who would be happy to murder every American—

indeed, does anyone doubt that bin Laden would have used nuclear weapons against the United States had he had access to them?—suggests to me that the people who carried out such attacks were profoundly evil and that those who raise banners supporting such actions are profoundly evil (or at least moral ignoramuses of the lowest order) as well.

Shortly after World War II, Golda Meir, later Israel's prime minister, met with a high-ranking British official (at the time, Britain ruled over Palestine). In the course of their meeting, the man commented in passing, "You must agree that if the Nazis persecuted the Jews, they must have had some reason for it." Mrs. Meir walked out and, to the man's utter astonishment, never spoke to him again (*My Life*, page 199).

I believe that her behavior was correct. Saying that the Jews were in some way responsible for the Nazis' hatred of and genocide against them is immoral. So, too, is it immoral to say that the hatred unleashed against America on September 11 is somehow America's fault.

I write this not as a naive defender of all that the United States does and has done. All people, Americans and non-Americans alike, have a right to be angry at American policies that they feel are wrong. But anger is one thing, hatred and murder another. A person who believes that it's right to murder an American for being an American demonstrates pathological hatred. And just as I would find it obnoxious and cruel to say, "What is it about America that could have so angered Charles Manson that he could order the brutal slaying of Sharon Tate and her friends?" so, too, do I find it outrageous to say that America needs to look into its soul because of the September 11 attacks. Rather, it is the terrorists and their supporters (and there are apparently many of them) who should ask themselves, "How can I claim to believe in God and treat other of God's children so cruelly?"

I want to make one additional point. Among the beliefs held by those who raised that banner was that one of the despicable features of American life is the equality granted to American women. As you are perhaps aware, Afghanistan under the Taliban allowed girls an education only to the age of eight, publicly lashed women teachers who violated this ban, and put other restrictions on women. Such restrictions on women's rights are features of countries controlled by fundamentalist Islam. Are we to understand, therefore, that because the world of radical Islam sees in the equal rights of American women a great evil that we should do some soul-searching and maybe reconsider the high status of women in America and the West?

People who believe that no Americans are innocent have told us something profoundly important about themselves: They are evil. If I want to do soul-searching, I'm likely do so when a good person points out something wrong that I have done, not when an evil person spews forth hate-filled invective against me.

Postscript: Sharp critiques of my position poured in. While the writers generally took pains not to justify the September 11, 2001, terrorist attacks, they took equal pains to insist that the United States had provoked them. As one characteristic letter argued, "Smoking two packs of cigarettes a day does not justify cancer. It does not make cancer a good thing. But it sure as hell causes cancer, and if smoking gives you cancer and you somehow beat the disease and then keep on smoking, you're the biggest fool in the world. In the same way, U.S. actions toward the Islamic world don't justify September 11 or make the murders good, but they sure as hell caused it and if we don't (to use a religious phrase) repent of our sins and change our ways, there will be future attacks and fuzzy-thinking people like you will bear a large part of the responsibility."

Significantly, writers like this take it for granted that U.S. behavior toward the Islamic world is so reprehensible that it need not even be documented. I have no idea what behavior he is talking about, and it's definitely hard to "repent" of one's sins if one doesn't even know what they are. This writer's assurance that such depth of hatred must be in response to reprehensible behavior on our side makes little sense. Does he believe that the mistreatment of women by the Taliban and in parts of the Muslim world prove that it was the bad behavior of women that has brought about such oppression?

Furthermore, U.S. actions toward the world of Islam hardly have been hateful. To cite one significant, but rarely noted, example: The last three times the United States deployed troops overseas, it was to *protect* Muslims: in defense of Muslims under attack in Kuwait (the Gulf War), to provide food to starving Muslims in Somalia, and in support of Bosnian Muslims being killed and persecuted by Serbian Christians.

I can only assume that people whose thinking is itself fuzzy (which is the kindest thing I can say about this writer) enjoy making this charge against others.

Dear Joseph,

I read an article ("Good Character Without Threat or Promise") in which Alan Dershowitz, the Harvard law professor, argued that secular people who risk their lives on behalf of a good cause are truly good and heroic people, because they do so with no expectation of reward. However, when religious people who believe in an afterlife sacrifice their lives for a good cause, they shouldn't be regarded as good or heroic. Rather, their action is the result of the pragmatic calculation that it's worthwhile to die as a martyr, since they will be rewarded with an eternity in heaven. As Dershowitz puts it, "I have never quite understood why people who firmly believe they are doing God's will are regarded as 'good,' even 'heroic.' For them the choice is a tactical one that serves their own best interests, a simple consequence of a cost-benefit analysis." His logic seems irrefutable. Do you agree?

Secular Is Better

Dear Secular Is Better,

Alan Dershowitz is a man for whom I have a lot of admiration. He is exceedingly bright, almost always provocative, and has supported many causes that I think are moral and important (the O. J. Simpson case and many of his periodic attacks on conservatives are, to my mind, exceptions). But in this instance I believe he is being naive and wrongheaded.

What, after all, is the implication of Dershowitz's line of reasoning—that a secular person who does something because he thinks it's right, even though he does not believe in an afterlife, is morally superior to one who does the same act and encounters the same suffering, but who also believes that he will be rewarded after death? Dershowitz obviously feels that the motives of the religious martyr are pragmatic and not pure, but what makes him certain that the motives of the nonbeliever are in fact pure? Perhaps it is very important to this person that he be regarded as a hero. Would that diminish the goodness of his deed? Dershowitz may think so, but I don't.

The most obvious implication of Dershowitz's reasoning is that religious people act well only because they believe in an afterlife. But how then does Dershowitz account for bad religious people (and I have no doubt that he believes there have been plenty of those)? The truth is, even religious people can't be sure whether there's an afterlife, or even whether there's a God. That's why we speak of *faith* in God. We don't say that people have faith that two plus two equals four; we have knowledge of that fact.

But when it comes to God and issues such as afterlife, people believe or don't believe. And while it is possible that people with deep faith have less fear of death than people with no faith at all, they usually do fear dying.

The New Testament attributes such fear even to Jesus, whom Christians regard as the most perfect person who ever lived, and whom Christianity views as both a man and god. According to the Gospel, Jesus, while suffering on the cross, cried out, "My God, my God, why have you forsaken me?" (Matthew 27:46). At that moment, he seemed to be afraid of death. One certainly doesn't have the impression that he was making a pragmatic calculation that dying in this awful way was a really good bargain.

I find it naive to claim that a religious person who loves his life and his family doesn't regret losing them when he sacrifices his life to do the right thing.

In 1973, I spent three weeks visiting political dissidents in what is now the former Soviet Union. One of the highlights of my trip was a three-hour meeting with Andrei Sakharov, the noble dissident who did so much to publicize the evils perpetrated by the Soviet leadership. He was one of the most distinguished scientists in the Soviet Union, and a wealthy man before he embarked on his campaign of protest. Sakharov's life was made miserable by Russia's Communist rulers. As became apparent during our discussion, Sakharov was not a believer in a God who judges and rules the world, and I consider him one of the great saints of our time. But I'm equally struck by the heroism of three rabbis, Menachem Zemba, Shimshon Stockhammer, and David Shapiro, the last rabbis in the Warsaw Ghetto during World War II. At one time, half a million Jews had been confined to the ghetto, but by 1943, the Nazis had murdered about 90 percent of them, and the Polish Catholic Church's leadership suddenly made it known that it was willing to smuggle out and save the lives of these three remaining rabbis. The rabbis met to consider this life-saving offer. Rabbi Shapiro spoke first: "We know well that we can no longer help our fellow Jews in any way. However, merely by being with them, by not leaving them, we encourage and strengthen them. It is the last possible encouragement that we can still give to the last Jews. I simply don't have the strength to leave these unfortunate people." All three rabbis refused to be saved (only Rabbi Shapiro survived the war).

I don't believe, as Dershowitz might argue, that these rabbis, deeply pious believers, made a pragmatic calculation to stay in the ghetto, die, and go to heaven, rather than save their lives. I suspect that they feared dying and might well have been tempted to save themselves. But they did the right thing, providing comfort and service to their fellow Jews. I regard Sakharov as a hero and these rabbis as heroes, and for the life of me I can't imagine why anybody would want to quibble and say that one was a greater hero than the others.

Dear Joseph,

I know the Bible instructs us to love God. That, I can accept. But to be honest, there's plenty in the Bible about fearing God. I've always hated that. What good can come from fear of God, except the creation of scared automatons who carry out meaningless rituals, or even ethical acts, in a state of terror?

Annoyed at the Bible

Dear Annoyed at the Bible,

Fear of God has gotten something of a "bum rap." Admittedly, it has sometimes been used by clergyman and theologians to terrify people and I, like you, find that abhorrent. But in the Bible itself, you'll find that fear of God is expected to make people morally better, both by helping to guarantee protection of the weak and by freeing people from fear of human beings.

Concerning protecting the weak, the injunction to "fear God" almost invariably follows laws that mandate the kind and fair treatment of people weaker than ourselves. For example, "You shall . . . not place a stumbling block in front of a blind person; you shall fear your God" (Leviticus 19:14). Why does the Bible add the words *you shall fear your God* to this commandment? Because even a sadist would be cautious before tripping another, if only out of concern that the person would see who had hurt him and seek vengeance. But one who trips a blind person has no reason to be afraid, because the victim won't know who hurt him. Thus, the Bible reminds us that when we have no reason to fear the victims of our acts, we must remember to fear God, who demands that we act justly.

Another example: "You shall not rule over [your servant] ruthlessly, but you shall fear God" (Leviticus 25:43). Throughout history, people have mistreated servants, and assumed, usually rightly, that there was nothing the servants could do about their oppression. Yet it is precisely because masters have no reason to fear servants that the Bible reminds them to fear God. The contemporary implication is that whenever you're dealing with a person in a weaker position than yourself—perhaps a nanny, handyman, or cleaning woman—and are tempted to take advantage of this imbalance, remember "And you shall fear God."

Fear of God also can liberate us from fear of human beings who are stronger than we are. Thus, the first chapter of Exodus records that the Egyptian Pharaoh ordered the midwives working with the Hebrews to kill all male babies immediately after delivering them. The midwives refused to do so because, the Bible tells us, they feared God (Exodus 1:17). Although the midwives presumably feared Pharaoh, they feared God even more. On the other hand, because other Egyptians feared only Pharaoh, they, unlike the midwives, followed Pharaoh's subsequent order to hunt down and drown the Israelite infants. Significantly, this biblical tale is the first story of civil disobedience in recorded literature. It reminds us that, in liberating us from fear of human beings, fear of God can enhance morality and save lives.

Dear Joseph,

In some comments of yours that I read on the sad fate of Daniel Pearl, the *Wall Street Journal* reporter who was kidnapped and murdered by Islamist terrorists in Pakistan [in January 2002], you were quoted as having said that we should pray for God to avenge Mr. Pearl's death. I assume you mean that we should pray that something bad will happen to the killers of this innocent man. But is not earthly justice man's, not God's, domain? Sure, I would like to see the barbarous killers brought to trial. But is it right to pray to God to harm another life? Should we not pray that these persons will be reunited with God's love?

Watch What You Pray For

Dear Watch What You Pray For,

Although earthly justice is man's domain, it often is hard to achieve. Therefore, one of the things for which I believe it right to pray is that God help ensure that earthly justice prevail. My hope is that Daniel Pearl's torturers and murderers be caught, tried, and severely punished, and so when I pray to God about this matter, my first prayer is that God will help bring this about.

The implication of your letter is that instead of offering such a prayer to God, I should pray instead that these men repent, whereupon they would be reunited with God's love, and presumably forgiven.

Your argument puts me in mind of T. S. Eliot's words, "After such knowledge, what forgiveness?"

Harsh though it may sound, I believe that there are some acts a human being commits that put him or her beyond, or close to beyond, the possibility of repentance. In my opinion, the extraordinary cruelty that these terrorists premeditated and perpetrated against Mr. Pearl places them into this category. As is the case with all human beings, his murderers were created in God's image. Unfortunately, they have, I believe, destroyed the image of God within themselves.

Your letter made me recall a question posed some years ago by Simon Wiesenthal, the concentration-camp survivor who devoted his post-Holocaust life to tracking down Nazi murderers and seeing to it that they were tried. In the 1970s, Wiesenthal published a book called *The Sunflower* (it is unclear whether the story is fiction, although he presents it as nonfiction). He relates how one day during his years in a Nazi work camp, he was taken from his work detail by a nurse, who took him to the bedside of a wounded Nazi soldier at a hospital in the camp.

After the soldier ascertained that Wiesenthal was a Jew, he confessed to him that in a town in Poland he had helped round up the Jews, brought them to their synagogue, and set the building on fire, killing all the people inside. Now that he was dying, this SS officer, who had been raised a Catholic but had long since abandoned his religion, realized what an awful thing he had done, and sought forgiveness from a Jew before he died. Could Wiesenthal find it in his heart to forgive him? Wiesenthal said nothing, and simply left the room.

Thirty years later, he sent out the story and asked others, including religious and political leaders, if he had been right not to forgive the man. One person to whom he sent the story was Cynthia Ozick, the well-known novelist and essayist. She noted in her response that "Graham Greene explains the Catholic idea of hell—no longer that endless site of endless conflagration; instead an eternal separation from God. Let the SS man die unshriven. Let him go to hell."

Now, Ozick is speaking of a person who at least expressed some contrition for what he had done. But in the case of which you are writing, it seems clear that Daniel Pearl's murderers regret only one thing: that they cannot do to many more Jews what they did to him.

Do I want God to avenge Daniel Pearl's death? Yes. Both in this world and in the next (i.e., through an eternal separation from God). I know that some people believe that God's love is infinite and that God bestows as great a love on the most evil as on the most good. Personally, I would find it hard to love or respect God if I believed that God equally loved Anne Frank and Adolf Hitler, or Daniel Pearl and his murderers, and ordained the same fate for all of them.

How then might God regard Pearl's murderers if they were to truly repent? There are limits to my presumptuousness; I don't know God's will. But in the past few years, and because of some unusual personal experiences, I have found myself drawn to the possibility of reincarnation. Perhaps, if such people truly repented, God would send them back into the world, and they might live lives in which they resisted evil and did a great deal of good. Perhaps several lifetimes of great kindness could undo one lifetime of unspeakable crime.

But such calculations must be left to God. In this world, I would feel much better knowing that all religions agreed on the desirability of teaching children that cruelty is evil and that the murder of innocent people is an unforgivable wrong. In other words, to teach people to repent before they commit irrevocable evil, not afterward.

Dear Joseph,

A friend of mine has become very drawn to the whole issue of reincarnation. She's reading through all the books of Brian Weiss [a Florida-based psychiatrist, and author of *Many Lives, Many Masters*] and has even been hypnotized to go into a previous life. Because I'm a religious person—my friend is, too—I wonder whether she should try to figure out whether she's lived before and will live again. The fact that God withholds such knowledge from our conscious minds suggests to me that it's not knowledge we need or should have. What good can come from trying to figure out if we've lived before or will live again?

Religious but Rational

Dear Religious but Rational,

A great deal of good, I would answer. Imagine, for example, that white Southerners who lived before the Civil War had been convinced that there is reincarnation. Realizing that they or their children might return to the world as blacks and as slaves, they might have started treating their own slaves very differently, and might even have freed them.

In short, a belief in reincarnation can motivate people to be more ethical, though it won't necessarily do so. I remember reading once that Gandhi complained that the belief in reincarnation in India sometimes restrained people from doing good. When they saw seemingly righteous people suffering, they assumed that these people were being punished for bad acts committed in a previous existence and, in consequence, were not moved to help them.

Such reasoning, however, strikes me as perverse. If you are indifferent to suffering, then you yourself are callous and may well be punished in your next lifetime.

Do I, like your friend, believe in reincarnation? I've had some experience with friends whose past-life recalls were filled with such a multitude of details—information I do not know how they could have discovered otherwise—that I find myself very open to believing that our souls have been here before, and will return. And I don't find that this belief conflicts, in any way, with my other religious beliefs. In addition, it helps explain things that otherwise seem inexplicable; why some human beings, for example, seem to come into the world with fears that have no relationship to their own experiences, why others have highly developed talents (such as being able to play the piano after few or no lessons), and why some people are drawn to groups other than their own when they are still very young.

I certainly have no desire to convince you to believe in reincarnation; I myself am still uncertain on the subject, although I lean toward belief in it. But I don't see any reason for you to be troubled by your friend's attraction to reincarnation. Now, if she started to believe in something truly irrational—for example, that she was destined to win the lottery if she only bought a hundred dollars' worth of tickets before each drawing—*that* would worry me.

Dear Joseph,

I saw my brother walking down the street the other day, his face flushed. He said he'd just gotten off the subway. After a train had pulled away from the station, a man—drunk, angry, and suicidal—jumped on the tracks. My brother stood frozen, wondering whether he should jump onto the tracks to help this guy get off. As my brother mulled over what to do, and used his cell phone to call for help, another man jumped onto the tracks, lifted the guy up, and put him back on the platform before another train could arrive. My brother was wracked with guilt, condemning himself for not jumping onto the tracks to help. Should he feel guilty?

Guilty or Not

Dear Guilty or Not,

Your letter recalls a debate in the Talmud: Two men are traveling together in the desert, and one has a pitcher of water. If both drink the water, they will both die, but if only one drinks, he can reach civilization and survive. What should the man with the water do? Rabbi Ben Petura taught, "It is better that both should drink and die, rather than one of them look on while his comrade dies." But Rabbi Akiva came and taught, "Your life takes precedence over his."

While the Talmud does not formally rule on this question, most commentators have sided with Rabbi Akiva: Your life takes precedence over that of another (the exception being that you are forbidden to kill an innocent person to save your life).

Akiva's reasoning certainly seems to apply in this case; your brother's life takes precedence over that of the would-be suicide. As I see it, the risk to your brother was substantial. Because the man was suicidal, he might well have resented and resisted any efforts to save him, and such resistance could easily have led to your brother's sharing his fate. Also, unless your brother is unusually athletic, it is no small feat to jump down onto a train track and pull up another (perhaps unwilling) adult.

Obviously, your brother was right to do what he could and try to summon assistance. Also, in such a case it would make sense to run to the front of the station and try to signal the conductor to stop, although I realize that once the train has started to pull into the station, it is unlikely to stop in time.

As regards the man who jumped down to save the man on the tracks, I am in awe of his courage and athletic prowess. If, however, he had died, God forbid, I wonder if his family members would have felt that his action constituted a worthwhile sacrifice of his life. I don't think it would have, and it is therefore by no means clear to me that he acted more morally than did your brother, though he assuredly acted more heroically.*

What about the person who jumped? Obviously, one feels sympathy for people who want to commit suicide. But I question the morality of someone who doesn't consider the effect his death will have on the person he, in effect, forces to kill him. I understand that some, perhaps many, people who commit suicide want to hurt someone whom they feel has hurt them. But to jump in front of a train, and leave the train engineer with a terrible, perhaps lifelong, legacy of

---

*I am in awe as well of firefighters who enter burning buildings to save lives, but that is part of the responsibility they assume when they choose their profession (although even in the case of firefighters, I don't think it would be fair to insist that they risk their lives, e.g., by climbing onto the ledge of a bridge to save a would-be suicide). But there certainly is no similar acceptance of responsibility when you pay your fare.

guilt, is a cruel thing to do. An alternative, such as taking an overdose of drugs, strikes me as a more moral way of ending one's life (though I consider suicide, in any but extreme cases, to be immoral).

So should your brother feel guilty? That he does reflects his essential goodness of character, but, in truth, he did nothing wrong, and there is no reason he should feel any guilt.

Dear Joseph,

In a recent letter, you mentioned that you almost always consider suicide to be immoral. Murder is immoral, because it takes the life of a person who doesn't want to die. But what is the moral issue in suicide? Why shouldn't a person have the right to end his or her own life if he or she no longer thinks it's worth living? Also, just out of curiosity, when you said that suicide is almost always immoral, what were the exceptions you were thinking of?

Pro-Choice

Dear Pro-Choice,

My perspective on moral issues is shaped by my religious convictions, one of them being that God created human beings in His image, and, in consequence, God is a partner in our lives. Therefore, when you kill a person, you are also striking out against God, in whose image every human being has been fashioned. And just as no other person has the right to kill you (since you are fashioned in the image of God), so, too, do you, for the same reason, lack the right to kill yourself.

On the other hand, I acknowledge that from a secular perspective, no convincing case exists as to why a person who wishes to kill himself shouldn't. One might tell him how much pain such an act will inflict on his family, how it is likely to cause those who love him to feel deep guilt, and maybe this will cause him to change his mind. Would-be suicides should further be reminded that suicide is often contagious, and family members of suicides are more likely than others to kill themselves (others argue that it is not an issue of contagion, but simply that clinical depression is hereditary). But if these arguments don't work, I don't know what *moral* argument (as opposed to a commonsensical one, such as "the unhappiness you're now feeling may soon pass") one can use to stop a person from committing suicide. Many secular people might even question the morality of trying to convince someone who wishes to die that he has no right to act on this wish.

Some years ago I got into an argument with an editor who was preparing to bring out a paperback edition of a book arguing on behalf of people's right to kill themselves. The book, which had received much notoriety when it was published in hardcover, included instructions on the least painful and messy ways in which to end one's life (I'm not mentioning the book's title because I don't want to encourage anyone to purchase it). I argued vociferously that it was wrong to publish such a book, to which she responded that human beings who want to die have the right to do so.

Realizing that religious arguments would not sway this woman, I asked her to consider that on any given day, there are probably thousands of teenagers who are thinking of ending their lives; the last thing I would want to put into their hands is a manual instructing them how to do this. For the overwhelming majority of these young people, the desire to die is a passing emotion, and one that they will later be very happy not to have acted on.

Similarly, many adults go through periods when they wish they didn't have to wake up the following morning. The problem provoking such despair could be a marital breakup, a financial collapse, or, as was the case with New York City's feisty former mayor Ed Koch, the questioning of one's integrity and character.

During Koch's mayoralty, a series of scandals rocked his administration. He realized that although he knew that he had done nothing dishonest, many people thought he had: "It was a very painful time. There were even moments when I thought seriously of killing myself. I really did. I thought about it in tactical terms, and I thought about it in spiritual terms. . . . If only I had a gun. Thank God I had convinced Bob McGuire [the police commissioner] to remove the gun from my bathroom safe all those years ago. If I had had it, at that vulnerable point, I really think I might have used it. A gun would have done the job nicely, cleanly, quickly. I think it's entirely possible that if I had a gun nearby, in the spring and summer of 1986, I would not be here today" (*Citizen Koch*, pages 212–213).

I'm happy Koch did not have access to that weapon, because I believe that suicide is profoundly wrong and that his death would have been a tragedy. So when, in response to your second question, do I think suicide is justified? The Bible, for example, records that when Israel's first king, Saul, was about to be captured by the Philistine army, he said to his arms-bearer, "Draw your sword and run it through me, so that the [Philistines] may not run it through me and make sport of me." The text tells us that his arms-bearer, in great awe of the king, refused to do so, "whereupon Saul grasped the sword and fell upon it" (I Samuel 31:4).

The Bible does not have many kind things to say about Saul during the demented last years of his king-ship, but neither the Bible nor biblical commentators condemn his suicide. As one commentator puts it, "It was better for him to take his own life rather than have the [Philistines] make sport with him."

In other words, I would argue that a soldier, a leader, or perhaps anyone who knows that he will be captured and tortured has the right to end his life. Thus, Jewish sources speak positively of several hun-dred young women who were captured by the Roman army—whose soldiers intended to rape them and turn them into prostitutes—who killed themselves.

I don't advocate that people in such situations *should* commit suicide, only that I understand, empathize with, and can't criticize those who do so. I also have great sympathy for anyone who commits suicide because she is suffering unbearable chronic pain, or because he has a disease such as Alzheimer's that will eventually reduce the individual to a vegetative state (as a rabbi, I wish to emphasize that this last comment is my personal view, and is opposed to traditional Jewish teachings, which would condemn suicide even when committed by someone with an irreversible degenerative disease who was undergoing great physical and/or emotional suffering).

In short, I regard suicide as wrong, except when someone is facing a torturous existence. God, I believe, has put us in this world with unique responsibilities. As Bachya ibn Pakuda, a medieval Jewish philosopher, taught, "A suicide is a sentinel who has deserted his post."

Dear Joseph,

In the New York–based *Amsterdam News* (August 10, 2000), a prominent African-American newspaper, Wilbert Tatum, the paper's publisher emeritus, attacked the Democratic Party's nomination of Senator Joseph Lieberman for vice president in 2000. Tatum argued that "Gore and his minions did it for the money. . . . Jews from all over the world, especially in

Europe, Africa, Israel and South America will be sending bundles of money . . . America is being sold to the highest bidder." I assume that you, like I, don't believe this statement to be true. Is a column like this, therefore, immoral, or just one person's political view?

Furious

Dear Furious,

As a rule, lies are immoral, and since Tatum's statement, which implies that Jews throughout the world were involved in a conspiracy ("America is being sold to the highest bidder") to purchase a vice presidential nomination for a Jew, is a lie, it is immoral. What makes the immorality particularly grotesque is that this is the sort of antisemitic lie that has a long and harmful history. The twentieth century witnessed the publication of such antisemitic tracts as *The Protocols of the Elders of Zion* and *The International Jew*, which claimed that Jews were involved in an international conspiracy to dominate the world and to rule over non-Jews, and which Hitler cited in justification of his policy of regarding all Jews as enemies of humankind.

Should Jews, who are harmed by the spread of such malicious falsehoods, be permitted to sue someone like Tatum? I would love to see Tatum try to prove the existence of a far-flung Jewish conspiracy to buy the nomination for Joe Lieberman. However, American law protects individuals, but not groups, from libel. Thus, if a journal published the medieval

305

canard that Jews murder non-Jews and use their blood to make matzoh for Passover—a malicious lie that throughout history has caused the murder of tens of thousands of Jews—the Jewish community could take no action. Only if the journal accused a particular Jew can that person seek damages. Since Tatum has chosen to make outlandish statements about Jews as a group, the organized Jewish community can do nothing about it other than protest. Indeed, the Anti-Defamation League's national director, Abraham Foxman, wrote a letter to the *Amsterdam News* denouncing Tatum's assertion as "invidious and an antisemitic canard employed by antisemites, racists, and conspiracy theorists through the centuries."

Still another moral issue worth considering: Tatum's wife, the former Susan Kohn, is Jewish. What should a person do if his or her spouse makes prejudiced comments about the group from which that person comes? Should the person leave the marriage? I would be interested to hear what she thinks about her husband's assertions.

When I first read about Tatum's accusation, I went out and bought the *Amsterdam News*. I was gratified to see that while his article appeared on page 12, the front page carried the headline BLACK DEMS PRAISE GORE'S CHOICE [of Joseph Lieberman], and the article that followed cited prominent black officials praising Lieberman's candidacy even as they pointed out areas of disagreement with him.

So when do critical statements about Jews (or

any group) cease being merely political views and become unfair and immoral? Negative statements become unfair and immoral when they are untruthful and are vicious, when they inflame people to feel animosity and hatred against innocent human beings.

᛭

Dear Joseph,

A friend just passed on to me the following e-mail, which shocked me: "Did you see the recent *Oprah Winfrey Show* on which Tommy Hilfiger was a guest? Oprah asked Hilfiger if his alleged statements about people of color were true. He's been accused of saying things such as 'If I had known that African-Americans, Hispanics, and Asians would buy my clothes, I would not have made them so nice,' and 'I wish those people would not buy my clothes—they were made for upper-class whites.' What did he say when Oprah asked him if he said those things? He said, 'Yes.' Oprah immediately asked Hilfiger to leave her show. Now let's give Hilfiger what he asked for— let's not buy his clothes. Boycott Hilfiger! Please pass this message along."

As a person devoted to influencing people to act more morally, I thought you'd want to post this e-mail and encourage others to act like my friend and me and start boycotting Tommy Hilfiger.

Very Mad

Dear Very Mad,

Sad to say, although you might see yourself as a very mad but moral hero, you yourself are acting immorally. If I followed your advice, I would be doing so, too. You see, what was transmitted to you via e-mail was simply a very nasty rumor.

Passing on rumors, as your friend and now you have done, is a tricky business. Most rumors are negative. After all, when was the last time you heard someone whisper, "Hey, did you hear so-and-so is really a nice person?" So if you pass on a nasty rumor and it turns out to be untrue, you have slandered someone. In your case, you have done something worse: You have also tried to drive him out of business, or at least cause him financial damage.

Your e-mail was not the first time I've been exposed to this Tommy Hilfiger rumor. Some time ago, a friend in Los Angeles sent me a letter similar to yours, also urging me to pass on the boycott request. I immediately doubted the e-mail's truth, unable to imagine that a businessman like Hilfiger, even if he were a bigot, would say things on television that would cause large numbers of people to boycott his business. After all, businessmen want to increase the number of people who buy their products, not alienate them.

Furthermore, if someone had actually gone on *Oprah* and made such a statement, it would have provoked so much media attention that I, and everybody else in America, would already have heard about it. So I was extremely skeptical, and in response to the request that I help promote a boycott of Hilfiger, I asked my friend to check into the rumor's truth.

She did so, and learned that Hilfiger's company had heard that such rumors had been circulating on the Internet for some time, information that horrified the company and Tommy Hilfiger himself. He's not a bigot, and indeed has gone out of his way to feature models of all ethnic backgrounds in his advertisements. Needless to say, Hilfiger is deeply pained that many people think him to be a bigot, as would you if people thought that about you.

Oprah herself became aware that this ugly rumor was circulating and actually announced on her show that this whole incident had never occurred: "Read my lips. Tommy Hilfiger was never on my show."

So the rumor you transmitted to me, and I assume to others, is false.

Now that you are aware of this, you, like all of us in such a situation, will probably defend yourself by saying, "But I thought it was true."

As we used to say when I was growing up in Brooklyn, "Big deal." That your intentions were pure is irrelevant. Drunk drivers don't become drunk so that they can get into their cars and kill people. But if you drink a lot of liquor and then drive, sooner or later, you are going to hurt someone. Similarly, if you pass on a lot of rumors, including nasty ones, some of them are going to turn out to be untrue. In the process, a good person's reputation will be damaged, and possibly destroyed. That your intention was not malicious is as irrelevant as the fact that a drunk driver doesn't plan to kill anyone. And lest you think I'm exaggerating, having your reputation as a good person destroyed is somewhat like being killed. That's why we call slandering or libeling "character assassination."

Therefore, what should you do the next time you hear a nasty rumor about someone? Check it out very carefully before you pass it on. Apply the Golden Rule: If somebody heard such a rumor about you, how carefully would you want him to check it out before he shared it? And if he passed it on without checking it out, how impressed would you be by his defense that he meant well?

P.S. As a first step, you should contact everyone whom you e-mailed about Tommy Hilfiger and tell them that you were in error; perhaps you should also send them a copy of what I've written you.

Dear Joseph,

What did you think of the Pope's prayer on September 11, 2002, the first anniversary of the attacks on the World Trade Center and the Pentagon: "We pray for the victims today, may they rest in peace, and may God show mercy and forgiveness for the authors of this horrible terror attack." I think that's going a little—actually a lot—overboard. Do you agree?

Against Being Too Forgiving

Dear Against Being Too Forgiving,

I have a high regard for many things that Pope John Paul II has done. He played a significant role in hastening the demise of Communism in Eastern Europe, particularly in his native Poland. And as a committed Jew, I remain touched by his precedent-shattering attendance at a synagogue service in Rome, by his repeated opposition to anti-Semitism, and by his openness to Jews. I myself had the honor of having a brief audience with him in 1980.

You may be anticipating a "but," and indeed I have one: Why should the Pope, or anyone for that matter, pray to God to show mercy and forgiveness to the most merciless people on planet Earth? Mercy and forgiveness, I assume, mean, among other things, a remission of punishment. So I have a question for the Pope. Does he believe, as I am under the impression Catholic doctrine teaches, that there is a place in another dimension of existence known as Hell? And if he believes that these Islamist murderers are not there, then whom does he believe is?

Murdering more than three thousand people, as these nineteen terrorists and their Al-Qaeda backers did, has inflicted suffering that will go on for decades. There are many hundreds of young children who will never know their fathers or mothers, who might well grow up in poverty or severely diminished economic circumstances, and whose lives will be permanently affected for the worse because of this act. There are thousands of women and men who have lost the loves of their lives, and many parents who will go to their deaths inconsolable over the loss of their children. And, as regards the moral record of the murderers, it gets worse. We have strong reason to believe that the sole regret of the perpetrators of this act (certainly the sole regret of their Al-Qaeda supporters) would be that they didn't kill many thousands more.

As far as we know, the last words heard by the more than two hundred doomed passengers on the four crashed planes were the cries of their murderers, *"Allahu Akhbar!"* ("God is great!") The God whom Al-Qaeda and its supporters believe is great is a God with moral values more akin to those of Adolf Hitler than to those of the God whom Pope John Paul II believes is great or, for that matter, the God whom moral Muslims believe is great.

Part of God's greatness, I believe, is that he is loving and just. To extend forgiveness and mercy to such cruel people certainly doesn't strike me as just or, for that matter, loving to their victims. Does the Pope expect those victims' widows and widowers and parents and children to share in his prayers for mercy and forgiveness? Why should they?

I am far more impressed with the prayer offered at Auschwitz in January 1995 by Elie Wiesel, on the fiftieth anniversary of the death camp's liberation: "Although we know that God is merciful, please God, do not have mercy for those people who created this place. Remember the nocturnal procession of children, and more children, and more children, so frightened, so quiet, so beautiful. If we could simply look at one, our hearts would break. But it did not break the hearts of the murderers."

If the Pope believes that human beings have no free will, and that people who carry out acts like these are predestined to do so, then his beseeching forgiveness for them makes sense. If they didn't consciously choose to act in this way, then it is unfair to punish them. But if the Pope believes, as I presume he does, that human beings have free will, then it does not make sense to me that special divine mercy should be extended to those who use their free will to inflict such misery on others.

There are plenty of people who are in need of, and deserving of, mercy and forgiveness. But not this band of murderers and their supporters. To pray, rather, that God treat them with justice—and I humbly leave it to God to determine what is just in such a case—would strike me as fair, right, and godly.

Dear Joseph,

I am disturbed and very distressed by wanting to express my absolute opposition to the war the United States began against Iraq while I still express my genuine love of this country and support for the troops who are executing this inexcusable invasion. How to reconcile the two?

Conflicted

Dear Conflicted,

During the bitter years of the Vietnam War, there were two major elements within the antiwar movement. One group, with which I identified, loved America and thought Communism, Ho Chi Minh, and the Vietcong were totalitarian, but also thought, for a variety of reasons, that the war was unwinnable and it was therefore morally wrong to send American troops to fight a war in which many of them (it turned out, well over 50,000) would die, pretty much for no reason.

There was, however, a second group in the antiwar movement, those whose opposition to the war was fueled by a deep animus toward the United States (some left-wing publications of the time spelled our country's name "Amerika" to convey the idea that the United States was Nazi-like). Many of these people expressed affection and admiration for Ho Chi Minh, the Vietcong, and much of the Communist world, and some even carried their anti-American message to Hanoi in person. It was this mind-set that so infuriated many Americans, including me, against these antiwar protesters. In truth, it seemed as though they hated America and loved her enemies.

Today, the litmus test of why one might oppose the war against Iraq (I support it) is one's attitude toward Saddam Hussein. If you find him a profoundly evil person, but nonetheless think that a war to remove him from power is unwinnable, or that too many innocent people will die, or that the threat to America posed by his weapons is nonexistent or vastly exaggerated, then there is, of course, no inconsistency between opposing the war and loving America.

However, if you fall into the camp of those who minimize Saddam's evil (the thinking of this camp is widely shared by people on the Left, particularly the far Left) or, God forbid, see moral equivalencies between the United States and Iraq, then I believe your opposition to the war suggests an anti-American bias. Therefore, I would like to share with you a few anecdotes about Saddam Hussein, drawn from a highly regarded source of modern scholarship, Professor Jonathan Glover's *Humanity: A Moral History of the Twentieth Century*. Glover, a philosopher, ethicist, and director of the Centre of Medical Law and Ethics at King's College in London, is certainly not a man of the Right, and I have no idea of whether or not he supports the war against Iraq. Yet in his book, he offers a number of examples of the evil behavior of Saddam Hussein dating back to Hussein's 1991 takeover of Kuwait. If you are of queasy stomach, skip over these anecdotes. But any person who opposes trying to bring this man down should read them:

- Ahmed Qabazard was a nineteen-year-old Kuwaiti who was held by the Iraqis after Hussein invaded Kuwait. An Iraqi officer told his parents that he was about to be released, and the mother prepared a lavish meal for him. When the family heard cars approaching, they went to the door. When Ahmed was taken out of the car, they saw that his ears, nose, and genitals had been cut off. He was coming out of the car with his eyes in his hands. Before he could reach the door, the Iraqis shot him, once in the stomach and once in the head, then instructed his mother to be sure not to move his body for three days.

- When Kurdish forces captured the city of Kirkuk, they found there a prison that had formerly held political prisoners of Saddam Hussein. In one of the cells, ear lobes were nailed to the wall. In another, a large metal fan hung from the ceiling; they learned that prisoners were attached to the fan and beaten with clubs as they twisted. One torture victim told a journalist that prisoners also were crucified, nails driven through their hands into the wall. A favorite technique of Saddam's torturers was to hang men from the hooks and attach a heavy weight to their testicles.

- A twenty-year-old pregnant woman who was arrested by Hussein's troops was repeatedly raped over a period of two months and then electrocuted. Before she died, her breasts were cut off and her belly sliced open.

- During Hussein's occupation of Kuwait, some of Hussein's troops killed a boy, then told the boy's family that they were obligated to reimburse them for the bullet used to kill their son.

- During Hussein's decades-long rule over Iraq, children have been encouraged to inform on parents, and men have been forced to take part in the execution of their sons and brothers.

This is the man whom America is now fighting against; in addition, of course, there is reason to believe that he is acquiring and developing biological and chemical weapons. If you think that America is wrong for warring against this man, you can of course still be a loyal and patriotic American who simply thinks that Saddam Hussein is evil but that America has no business trying to drive him from power (if you do indeed believe that, however, I don't know how you can fulfill the words in your letter about expressing your "support for the troops who are executing this inexcusable invasion"). But anyone who, driven by great antagonism toward the American administration, tries to draw a moral equivalence between Saddam Hussein and the United States is, in my view, a scoundrel.

About the Author

JOSEPH TELUSHKIN, spiritual leader and scholar, is the author of the acclaimed *The Book of Jewish Values* and also *Jewish Literacy*, the most widely read book on Judaism of the past two decades. Another of his books, *Words That Hurt, Words That Heal*, was the motivating force behind Senate Resolution 151, introduced by Senators Joseph Lieberman and Connie Mack in 1996, which would have established a "National Speak No Evil Day" throughout the United States.

Rabbi Telushkin is a senior associate of CLAL, the National Jewish Center for Learning and Leadership, and the rabbi of the Los Angeles–based Synagogue for the Performing Arts; he also serves on the board of the Jewish Book Council. He lives with his family in New York City, has an ethics column on Beliefnet.com, and lectures regularly throughout the United States.